Taylor's Weekend Gardening Guides

Frances Tenenbaum, Series Editor

HOUGHTON MIFFLIN COMPANY
Boston • New York 1997

Easy, Practical Pruning

Barbara Ellis

Techniques for Training Trees, Shrubs, Vines, and Roses

For information about this and other Houghton Mifflin trade and reference books and multimedia products, visit The Bookstore at Houghton Mifflin on the World Wide Web at http://www.hmco.com/trade/.

Library of Congress Cataloging-in-Publication Data

Ellis, Barbara W.
Easy, practical pruning : techniques for training trees, shrubs, vines, and roses / Barbara Ellis.
p. cm. — (Taylor's weekend gardening guides)
Includes index.
ISBN 0-395-81591-6
1. Pruning. I. Title. II. Series.
SB125.E47 1997
635.9′1542—dc21 97-1775

Printed in the United States of America

WCT 10 9 8 7 6 5 4 3 2 1

Book design by Deborah Fillion
Cover photograph © by Saxon Holt

Contents

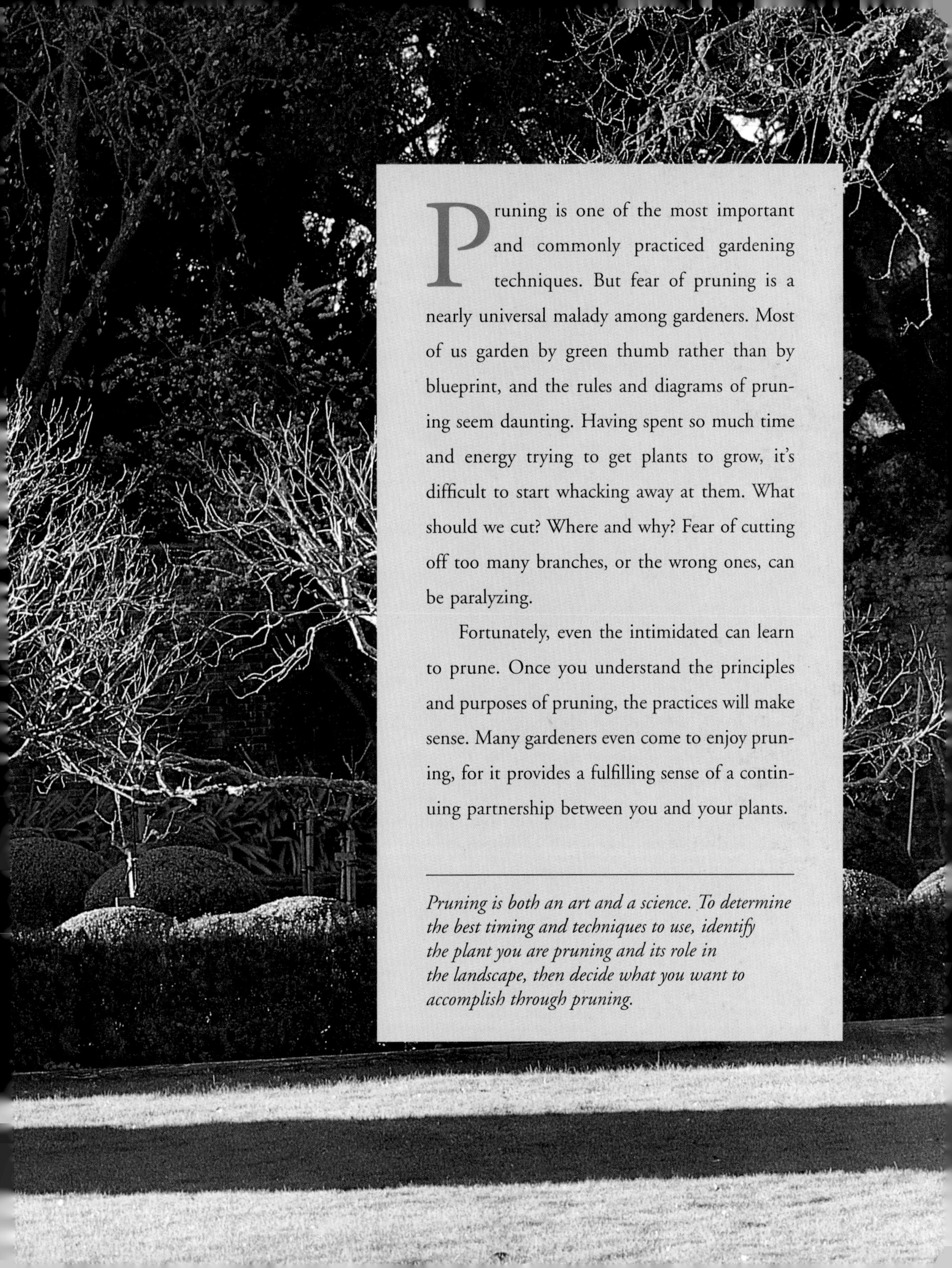

Pruning is one of the most important and commonly practiced gardening techniques. But fear of pruning is a nearly universal malady among gardeners. Most of us garden by green thumb rather than by blueprint, and the rules and diagrams of pruning seem daunting. Having spent so much time and energy trying to get plants to grow, it's difficult to start whacking away at them. What should we cut? Where and why? Fear of cutting off too many branches, or the wrong ones, can be paralyzing.

Fortunately, even the intimidated can learn to prune. Once you understand the principles and purposes of pruning, the practices will make sense. Many gardeners even come to enjoy pruning, for it provides a fulfilling sense of a continuing partnership between you and your plants.

Pruning is both an art and a science. To determine the best timing and techniques to use, identify the plant you are pruning and its role in the landscape, then decide what you want to accomplish through pruning.

CHAPTER 1: PRUNING FUNDAMENTALS

Most people think of pruning as removing limbs from a tree or branches from a shrub, but any time you take shears to a plant you are actually pruning. Removing spent flowers, cutting roses, pinching back perennials, and shearing herbs are all forms of pruning.

All types of pruning cuts, large or small, will induce or suppress plant growth. Understanding what causes growth and how pruning can direct it will make you a more efficient and effective pruner. A great many factors affect growth — sunlight, nutrients, water, temperature, pathogens, plant hormones, and genes. Of principal interest to the pruner is the role of the hormones called auxins in controlling growth. Auxins, which are produced continuously in the growing tips of shoots, promote growth at the tip while inhibiting the growth of buds along the sides of the shoot. The process by which a shoot tip controls growth is called api-

The period from late winter to very early spring, when plants are still dormant, is an ideal time to prune many deciduous trees and shrubs. Plant forms are easy to see and sculpt before the leaves emerge, and pruning wounds will heal quickly in the spring.

cal dominance, that is, the dominance of the apex, or tip. If you remove a growing tip, thereby cutting off its production of auxins, the previously dormant buds along the shoot just behind the tip, called lateral buds, will grow and become side shoots, or laterals. The topmost bud on the top side shoot will then become dominant and suppress the growth of buds below it. In many cases the topmost bud also becomes dominant over existing branches below it on the original stem, thereby slowing their growth, too.

Pruning and Apical Dominance

The process called apical dominance allows the tip of the stem to grow longer while suppressing growth of the buds below it on the stem.

If the tip of the stem is removed, eliminating the dominant bud, the previously dormant buds below it will sprout and grow.

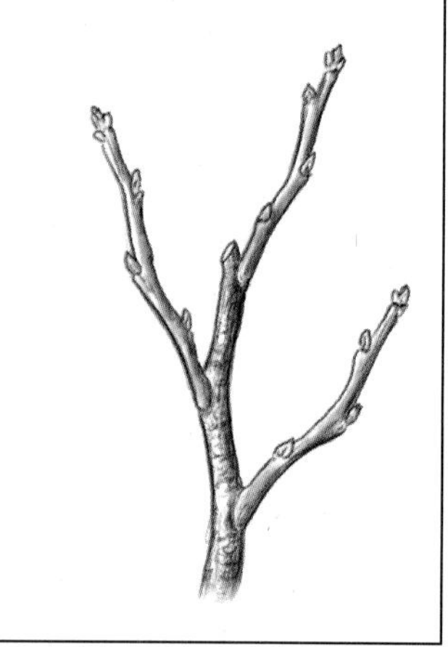

It's not hard to see, then, that whether you are pinching the leading shoots of snapdragon seedlings, shearing a privet hedge, or cutting back canes of a rosebush, you are directing the plant's growth by manipulating apical dominance. In each case the result is a bushier, more densely branched plant. Apical dominance also governs root growth: pinching out the tip of a root encourages branching, just as it does with shoots.

Along with encouraging branching, cutting off the tip of a branch or shoot also stimulates growth, even if that isn't your intention. In fact, shearing back a hedge or cutting back branches on a foundation shrub actually causes a flush of new growth.

Removing the branches below the tip, along the stem itself, has a different and generally less pronounced effect on growth: it increases the vigor of the tip and reduces future lateral growth.

TYPES OF PRUNING CUTS

Whether you are pruning an evergreen, an apple tree, a flowering shrub, or a vine, there are only two basic types of cuts: heading cuts and thinning cuts. These two cuts manipulate growth in different ways and are used for different reasons.

Heading Cut. This cut is made across a branch to remove the stem tip. The branch should be cut just above a bud or a side branch, ideally at a 45-degree

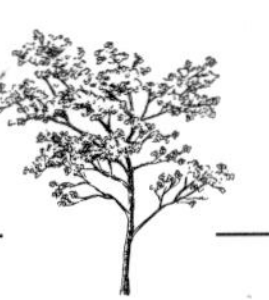

angle *away* from the bud. (On plants with opposite leaves, however, the cut should be straight across.) Since buds will grow in the direction they are pointing, in most cases you should prune just above a bud that points to the outside of the plant to encourage a spreading habit and keep the center of the plant open. (On plants with opposite leaves, you can rub off the bud that is pointing into the center of the plant.) If a shrub needs more growth in the center, prune above an inward-pointing bud.

Because a heading cut removes the dominant tip, it stimulates growth and encourages branching along the stem that has just been pruned. When you shear a hedge or shrub, you're actually making a series of heading cuts, even though hedge clippers don't make 45-degree cuts just above buds. Formal hedges require frequent pruning to keep them looking neat because shearing stimulates new growth.

Heading cuts will have different effects on different plants because apical dominance is much stronger in some plants than in others. Shrubs that are naturally heavily branched, for example, barely show apical dominance. Experience and observation will show you how the plants in your own landscape respond to heading cuts.

A Proper Heading Cut

Align the bottom of the cut as shown and slant it upward at a 45-degree angle to keep excess moisture away from the bud.

Heading Cuts for Opposite Leaves

On plants with opposite leaves, cut straight across the stem just above a strong pair of buds.

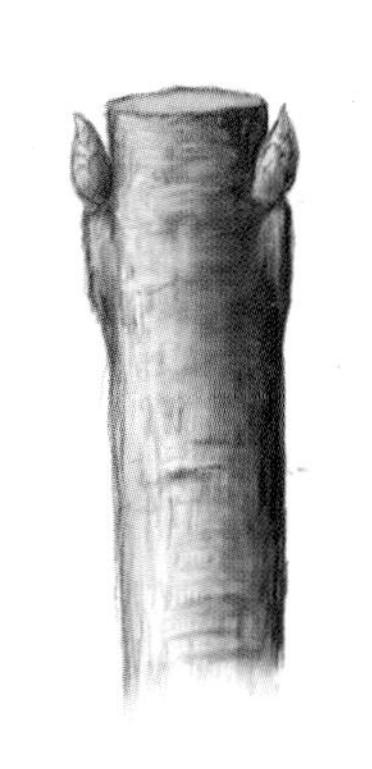

Thinning Cut. This cut removes a branch or shoot where it arises from a larger branch or the trunk of the tree. A proper thinning cut is made just outside the branch collar, the slight bulge at the base of the branch. (Leaving the branch collar intact promotes healing of the wound.) Depending on the size of branch or shoot you are removing, a thinning cut can be made with pruning shears, loppers, or a saw.

Use thinning cuts to remove dead and damaged growth, to open up the center of a plant to let in light and air, and to eliminate rubbing or crossing branches. By removing large branches and leaving smaller ones, you can also reduce the size of a shrub without stimulating the rampant growth that repeated shearing induces. Although thinning cuts do not cause a flush of new growth the way heading cuts do, they do tend to invigorate the buds remaining on the plant because the roots are supporting less top growth.

You can use thinning cuts to remove stems from overcrowded shrubs; simply cut them off at the base of the plant or as close to the ground as possible. This type of thinning cut is often used on flowering shrubs and roses to remove old wood that is no longer blooming well. Thinning out old wood generally causes the plant to produce vigorous new growth.

To make a proper thinning cut on a large limb, use a saw to make a three-step cut, as shown on page 7. This will remove the branch with a minimum of damage to the plant. If you simply cut right through the branch without first reducing its weight, the wound may not heal well. That's because once the branch is partially severed, it will fall, splintering the wood and tearing bark off with it. A three-step cut leaves a smooth wound that will heal much more quickly.

Reasons for Pruning

Understanding why you want to prune a plant is nearly as important as using the correct cuts. If you can begin with specific goals in mind, not only will you prune more effectively, you'll also have a better idea what cuts to make. Here are some of the main reasons for pruning.

Using Thinning Cuts

Use thinning cuts to remove branches without inducing new growth. Thinning cuts are the best way to open up the center of a plant, remove old wood to make room for new growth, and get rid of dead or broken branches.

Thinning Small Branches

To remove small branches, make thinning cuts close to the trunk or branch, but just outside the branch collar.

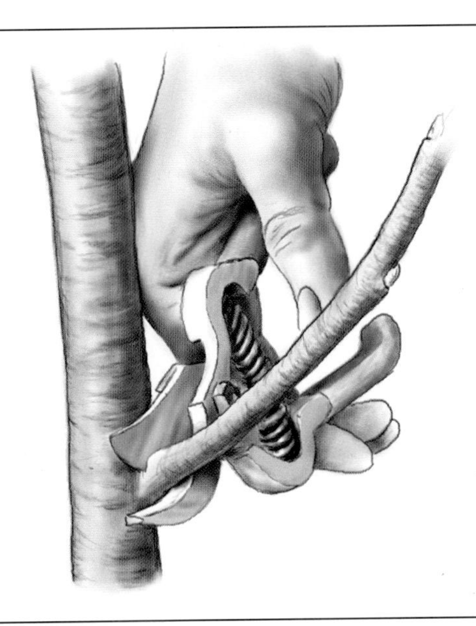

Removing Large Branches

Always remove large branches using the three cuts shown here. The first two cuts reduce the weight of the branch by cutting it off 6 inches or more from the trunk. The final cut severs the limb cleanly just outside the branch collar.

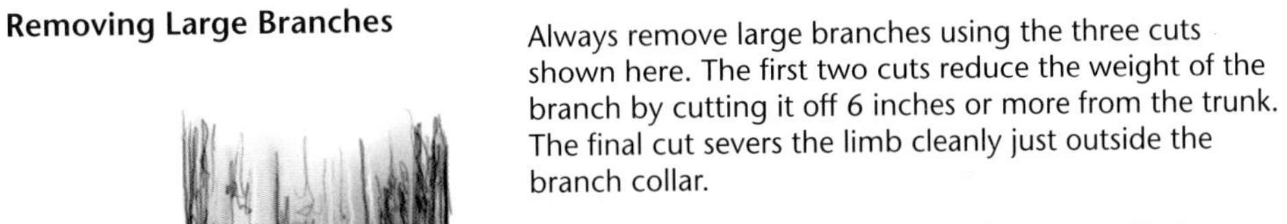

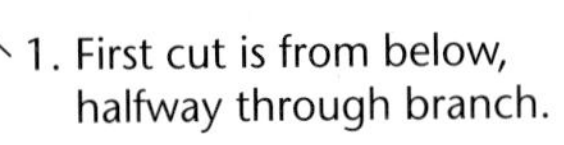

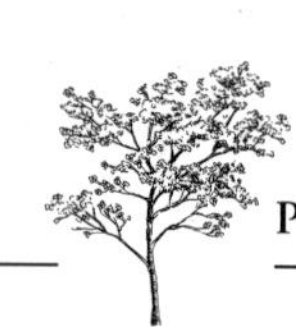

Remove Dead, Dying, Diseased, or Infested Wood. Probably the most important reason for pruning is to remove dead or dying wood on a plant by cutting back to healthy tissue. Broken branches should be cut also; not only can they be dangerous if they fall, but jagged, irregular wounds do not heal as easily as cleanly pruned wood does.

Pruning also is an effective way to control diseases. Remove all branches infected with a disease such as fire blight, cutting back to healthy wood and discarding or burning the diseased wood promptly.

Surprisingly, pruning is an easy, chemical-free way to control infestations of some insects, such as certain types of borers, which tunnel through branches or stems. Simply cut the branch back to healthy wood. By cutting off branches infested with a pest such as scale, you may be able to stop an infestation before it spreads to the entire plant.

Eliminate Crossing and Rubbing Branches. Branches that cross the center of a plant usually produce unattractive, congested growth. They also keep light and air from reaching the center of the plant and can foster conditions that promote disease. Branches rubbing against each other create wounds through which diseases and insects can enter; remove one of the branches with a thinning cut.

Promote Fast Healing

Even though pruning can be beneficial to plants, a pruning cut is still a wound, which can open the way to disease or insect infestation. Making sure that the wound heals quickly will help keep the plant vigorous and healthy. The best way to ensure rapid healing is to make the proper cuts with clean, sharp tools. When making thinning cuts, leave the branch collar intact, for it plays an important role in healing. Smooth, even cuts heal faster — and look more attractive — than jagged ones. Late winter to very early spring is a good time to prune many plants because wounds heal most quickly at that time of year. Pruning after the buds break, from spring through early summer, isn't generally advisable because the bark is easily torn during this period of fast growth. Plants that are healthy and well supplied with nutrients and water suffer few problems from judicious pruning.

Proper and Improper Pruning

To do a good pruning job, have clear goals in mind and use proper pruning cuts. Before you start, look at the plant carefully to identify existing problems. Also look for future problems you can prevent with corrective pruning now.

Correct pruning: The goal of pruning this shrub is to remove congested growth from the center and to encourage the development of a more open, vase-shaped habit.

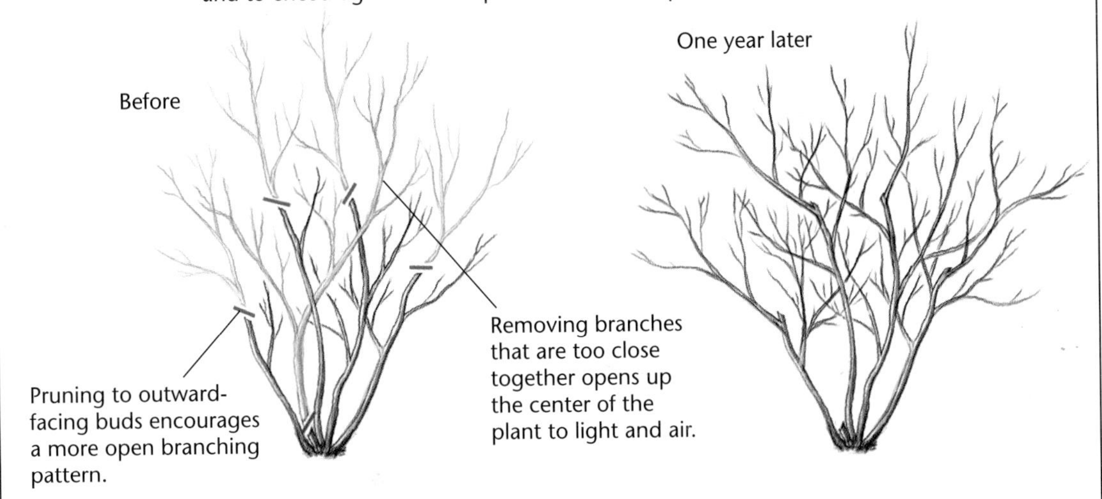

Incorrect pruning: With the same shrub, misdirected cuts can result in more serious problems and a less pleasing shape.

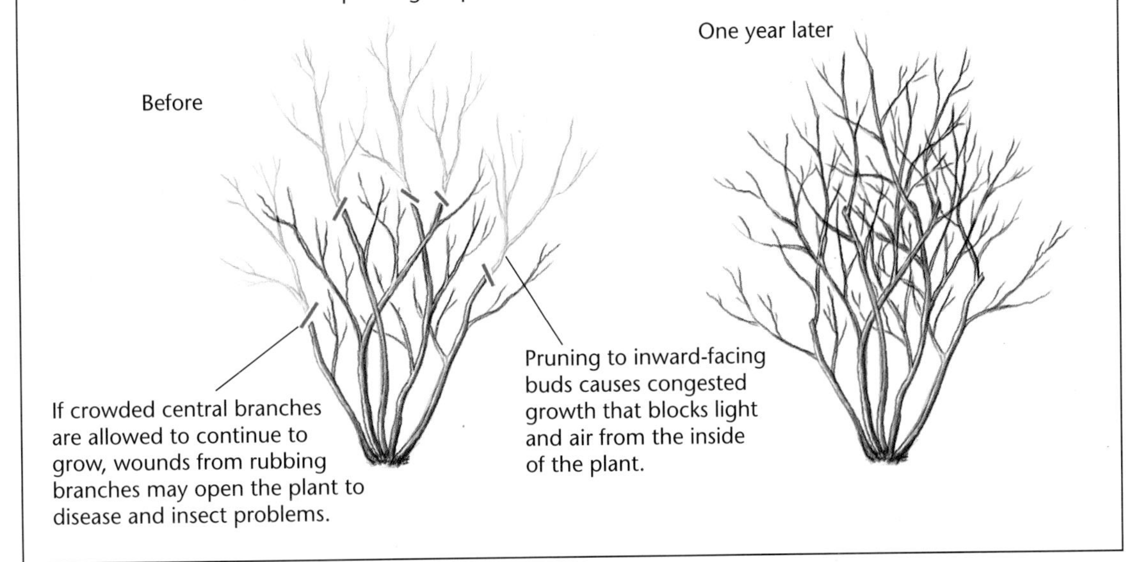

Improve Plant Shape. An important reason for pruning is to shape plants in a variety of ways to make them more attractive. To correct the shape of a lopsided shrub, for example, shorten overly long branches with heading cuts and remove wayward growth with selective thinning cuts. If your idea of an attractive shrub is a formal rectangle or globe, you'll need to shear it regularly to achieve the shape you want. For a lower-maintenance option, though, consider using thinning cuts and selective heading cuts to create a more natural shape.

Pruning can be used to create dense growth or to open up a plant so it serves as a delicate screen. For a hedge, dense growth is a necessity: whether you are growing a formal sheared hedge or are aiming for a more natural shape, use heading cuts to encourage branching. You can also use heading cuts to encourage thick growth on trees or shrubs that were planted to provide privacy to a backyard.

Use thinning cuts to open up a plant and let in light and air. This technique will result in a planting that frames but doesn't block a view beyond your property. Or remove a branch from a shade tree to reveal a view of the garden from your bedroom window.

Remove Unwanted Growth. Removing excess twiggy growth on a shrub or tree will redirect the plant's energy into more vigorous framework branches. Use thinning cuts also to remove growth that is crowding the center of a plant, including water sprouts on apples and crab apples. (A water sprout is a thin, unbranched, fast-growing stem growing vertically from a branch.) Not only are water sprouts unattractive, they block light and air and generally do not bear fruit. You should also use thinning cuts to remove reverted growth, such as fast-growing shoots on otherwise dwarf conifers, suckers arising at the base of a tree trunk, and root suckers that grow from the rootstock of a grafted rose, for example.

Train New Trees. In the first few years of growth, young trees require basic pruning to establish an attractive and sturdy framework of strong, healthy branches. Good early pruning will eliminate many problems that can occur once the tree becomes mature, such as weak branch crotches, which can break during windstorms, and awkward branching. Rigorous early training is especially important for fruit trees, which must have a sturdy framework of branches that will support a heavy load of fruit (see Chapter 3: Pruning for Fruits and Berries).

Removing Reverted Growth

Harry Lauder's walking stick (*Corylus avellana* 'Contorta'), grown for its twisted, contorted branches, is usually grafted onto the species *(Corylus avellana).* The rootstock often sends up uncontorted branches, which must be removed; otherwise they will overwhelm the grafted plant.

Widening a Narrow Crotch

Branches that meet the trunk at less than a 45-degree angle tend to be weak and may split under a heavy load of fruit or during a high wind. To train and strengthen branches of a young tree, spread narrow crotches to more than a 45-degree angle with wooden spacers. If branches are long and flexible, you can widen the angles by tying the branches to stakes.

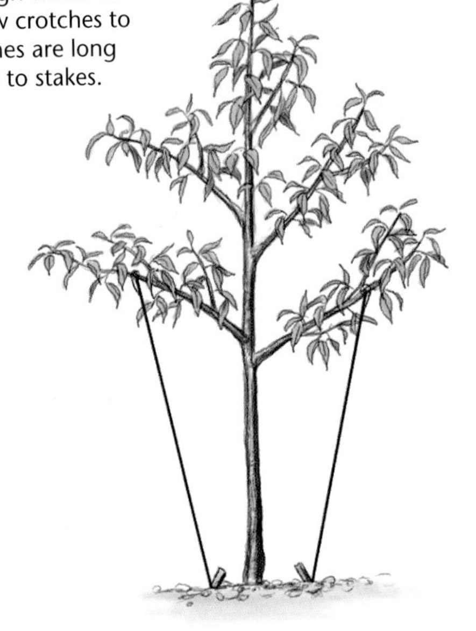

Improve Fruiting and Flowering. On many plants, judicious pruning will encourage abundant flowers and fruit. Thinning out older wood directs the plant's energy into the production of new growth and makes room for younger stems to grow. Newer wood generally bears more flowers and fruits than wood that is several years old. On shrubs such as roses, removing weak, twiggy growth and shoots that are too small to bloom also redirects energy and nutrients into the more vigorous growth that produces most of the flowers.

Eliminate Obstacles and Hazards. Generally, this type of pruning applies to shade trees. Use thinning cuts to eliminate low-hanging branches that may block a pathway as well as to remove deadwood that might fall and damage property or harm people. Also prune to eliminate weak, narrow branch crotches, which tend to break under stress. It's best to hire a professional arborist for most shade-tree pruning chores.

TIPS FOR SUCCESS

CONSIDER REMOVAL

Sometimes it is better to remove a plant than to try to prune it. If pruning a plant down to manageable size will destroy its appearance and health, or if you have to prune harshly every year to keep it in bounds, you are generally better off replacing it. To eliminate future pruning nightmares, always read the label or ask the nursery owner how big the plant will be at maturity. When you plant, give it ample room to grow. If you have limited space, look for dwarf cultivars that will not overgrow their space. Not only will you end up with more attractive plants, you'll have less pruning to do for years to come.

Reduce Plant Size. You may want to control the size of a plant that is blocking a window or door, has outgrown its place in a foundation planting, or is crowding out nearby plants in a shrub border. Gardeners commonly resort to shearing in these situations; they cut the plant back to the desired height, only to find that it quickly regrows. On a shrub you can use thinning cuts to remove the oldest and tallest branches, pruning them either to a few inches above the ground or to where they join a larger branch; evergreens and deciduous trees generally won't tolerate this practice, however. Some shrubs can be simply cut to the ground and allowed to regrow; others won't recover from such a drastic pruning process.

Deciding When to Prune

Figuring out when to prune a plant can be confusing, but there are some simple guidelines you can follow. Remove dead or dying wood any time you see it. Not

The best time for pruning flowering shrubs and trees — as well as fruits and berries — depends on whether they bear their flowers on new or old wood. Magnolias, such as 'Betty', at left, produce flowers on the previous year's growth and should be pruned immediately after they bloom.

only is deadwood a potential hazard, it may harbor plant diseases or insects that can further damage the plant. Always cut away broken branches cleanly whenever they occur as well.

New Wood or Old? In many cases, the best time to prune depends on whether the plant blooms on new wood or old. New wood is growth produced in the current season; old wood is that from the previous season or seasons. Plants that bloom on new wood are pruned during the dormant season. These include hybrid tea and grandiflora roses, butterfly bush (*Buddleia* spp.), and beautyberry (*Callicarpa* spp.).

Plants that bloom on old wood produce new flower buds for the following year shortly after the current season's flowers fade. Most popular spring-blooming shrubs fall into this category, including azaleas and rhododendrons, forsythia, and mock oranges (*Philadelphus* spp.). Prune them in late spring or summer, no more than a month after they flower. Otherwise you risk cutting off all of next year's flower buds.

Dormant-Season Pruning. Most plants should be pruned when they are dormant. Trees and shrubs pruned in dormancy will grow with renewed vigor in spring because they have proportionally more roots and food reserves for the remaining top growth. Another advantage of dormant-season pruning for deciduous plants is that the plant's framework is clearly visible, making it easy to see what pruning should be done.

For best results try to do your dormant-season pruning in late winter or very early spring. Pruning cuts heal faster in spring than in other seasons, minimizing the amount of time the plant has unhealed wounds. Another advantage is that you avoid exposing fresh pruning cuts to the most severe winter weather.

Growing-Season Pruning. Pruning in late spring and summer has advantages, too, and not just for plants that bloom on old wood. During the growing season you can easily direct new growth with a minimum of stress on a plant. Simply pinch out shoot tips to encourage branching or remove excessive twiggy growth to direct the plant's energy into developing its main scaffold branches, for example. It's best to prune evergreens in spring or summer when they are actively growing.

Keep in mind that pruning during the growing season tends to reduce a plant's vigor. For this reason summer is a good time to prune to reduce a plant's size. It is also the best time to remove unwanted growth such as water sprouts and suckers.

PRUNING TOOLS

Pruning can be done with anything from fingernails to a chain saw. Most gardeners rely primarily on pruning shears, but loppers and a pruning saw are handy for branches that are too big for shears. Maintaining a formal hedge or sheared shrubs requires hedge shears.

Here's a rundown of the basic pruning tools you should have in your arsenal.

Pruning Shears. These come in two basic designs, bypass and anvil. Bypass shears cut like scissors; a sharp convex cutting blade slides past a blunt, hooked concave blade that supports the stem being cut. Anvil shears, on the other hand, cut like

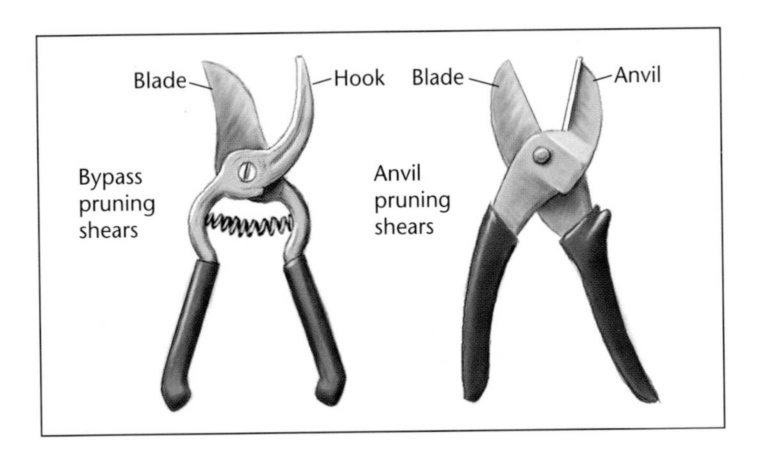

a knife on a cutting board: a straight blade cuts against a flat metal surface, the anvil, which also supports the stem. Bypass shears tend to damage a stem less than anvil shears; they're also better for reaching into tight spots. Anvil shears, however, are more powerful. Avid gardeners will probably want a pair of each type.

Hand shears come in a great range of models and prices, including designs for large and small hands and for left-handers. They should feel comfortable in your hand, and you should be able to operate them with ease. Choose a smaller pair if you can't grasp both handles without stretching or straining your hand. If you have weak hands, consider shears with a ratchet mechanism. (These, too, can crush stems, especially when used on stems that are too thick.) Inexpensive shears are serviceable for gardeners who prune occasionally, if the blades are kept sharp and properly adjusted, but you'll probably be more satisfied if you buy the best pair you can afford. Several models with replaceable blades are available through catalogs and better garden centers; these will last a lifetime with good care.

Examine the blades closely when purchasing shears. As you slowly close bypass shears, make sure that the cutting blade is in constant contact with the hook as it slides past. On anvil shears, the blade and anvil should be in contact along their full length when closed. If you regularly work with gloves on, remember to wear them when you try out hand shears before buying.

Loppers. These are essentially heavy-duty bypass or anvil shears attached to long handles. Requiring two hands to use, they provide considerable leverage and cutting power; some can handle branches up to 2 inches in diameter. Gardeners with

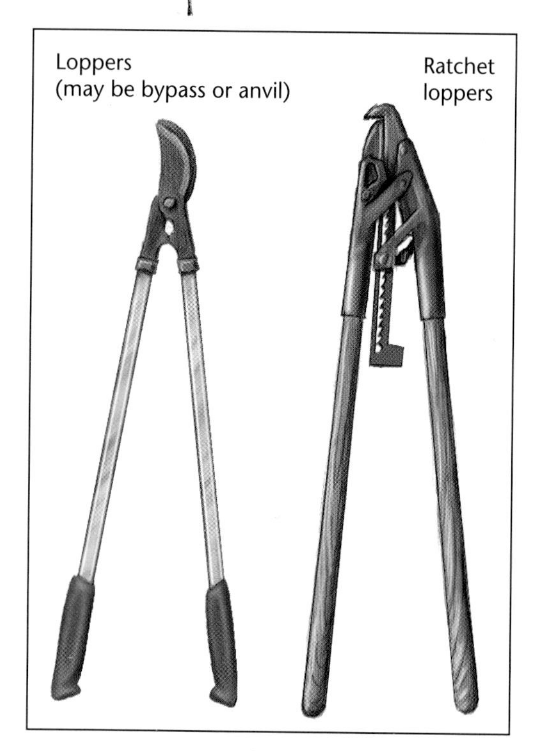

small or weak hands or stiff joints may find loppers easier to use than shears. There are ratchet models, too, although these can be difficult to use in close quarters — in the dense growth at the base of a large shrub, for example. Loppers, especially ratchet types, will crush the wood if they're used on a branch that is too thick. If in doubt, use a saw. Loppers also can be expensive, and there is nothing they do that can't be done with either hand shears or a saw. But if you maintain a lot of trees and shrubs, a good pair of loppers will save you time and work.

Saws. Two types of saws are useful for a variety of pruning jobs — frame saws and pruning saws. Frame saws are good for maintaining fruit trees and occasionally for pruning other trees and shrubs. There are many models on the market. Most have a lightweight tubular frame that supports and provides tension to a narrow, hardened-steel replaceable blade. A sharp frame saw will easily handle limbs up to 4 or 5 inches in diameter.

A pruning saw is an almost indispensable tool. It usually consists of a hardened-steel blade up to about 2 feet long attached to a wooden or metal handle. Because there's no frame to get in the way, a pruning saw can get into tight spots, and it is capable of handling limbs almost as big as those that a frame saw will cut. For especially tight spots, such as around the base of a crowded shrub, a pruning saw with a blade less than 1 foot long is useful. Pruning saws come in many models, with straight or curved blades as well as with different sizes and designs of teeth. Most cut in one direction only, generally on the pull stroke, or draw; some types cut on both the push and pull stroke, a useful feature in tight spots when you can move the blade only a few inches in either direction. Folding saws, with a blade that folds into the handle, are especially handy. They can be carried safely with other gardening tools and unfolded whenever they're needed.

Chain saws can be used to take down old trees or remove very large limbs, but in inexperienced hands they are seldom helpful pruning tools. They are

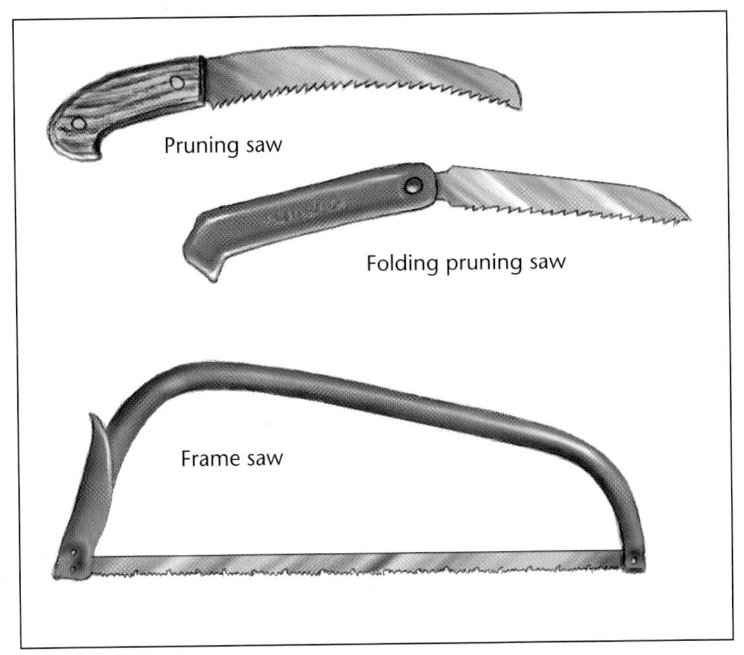

difficult to control when cutting, and often create tree wounds that will not heal properly. They are also quite dangerous, particularly if the user is perched on a ladder or a branch. Unless you've had a lot of experience, leave chain-sawing to professional arborists. Never climb a ladder to use a chain saw or hold it higher than your chest to make a cut.

Hedge Shears. If you have to maintain formal hedges or clipped foundation plants, hedge shears, either manual or electric, will come in handy. Use them only to cut succulent new growth. Use conventional pruning shears for thicker, hardened growth.

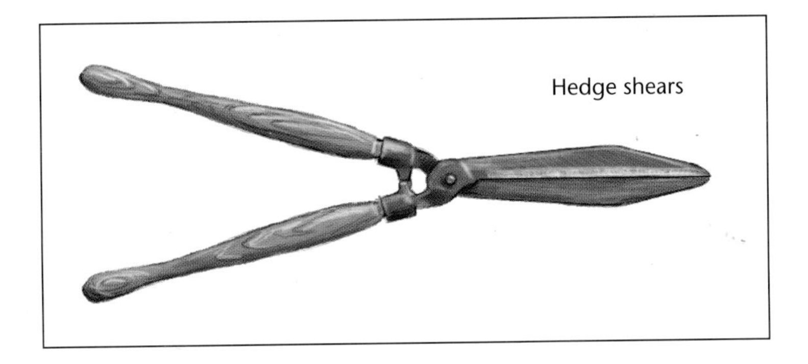

Safe, Efficient Pruning

Improper or inefficient handling of tools can produce fatigue and injury. Conversely, moving economically and using the right tool for the job in the most effective position will minimize problems and maximize work output. The tips listed below will help you learn to prune efficiently, effectively, and safely.

- Work close to your body, at a bent arm's length. Don't try to apply force to a hand tool or control a power tool with your arms at full length or reach up with your back arched or extended.
- Wear appropriate protective gear, including safety goggles, sturdy shoes, clothing that is comfortable but not baggy, and a hat.
- Select a tool that fits you physically — left-handed rather than right-handed clippers, for example — with handles of a size and shape that feel right. You will frequently have to prune with gloves on for protection against blisters, winter cold, thorns, and other hazards, so wear the gloves when you're choosing your pruning shears. Be sure that the tool can be opened and closed fully and easily and that the handles don't pinch your hand or glove.
- To reduce the chance or the severity of elbow and wrist strain, always try to operate hand clippers with your wrist straight and your elbow bent, especially if you are pruning tough wood for extended periods.
- Use your free hand to flex the branch slightly away from the cutting edge of your pruning tool, thus opening a kerf (groove), to make a smoother and easier cut. Open a kerf when using clippers as well as saws — especially anvil shears, which can crush tender stems.
- When using pruning shears or loppers, position the blade so that it cuts at about a 45-degree angle. Always cut back to live wood; make your cut just above an outward-facing shoot or bud, and never force or twist the blades when cutting.
- When using an extension tool such as a pole pruner, space your hands at least 2 feet apart on the handle. This will increase your control of the tool and lessen the strain.
- Plan your work for economy of motion, minimizing changes of position and shifts of the tool. But try not to stay in one position so long that your muscles become stiff.
- If you are going to use several tools in one pruning session, it's helpful to purchase or devise a system of holsters, belt hooks, and slings that will keep the tools accessible and safe.
- Know your limitations. Don't overestimate your stamina, tolerance of sun or heat, or skill; once you reach your personal threshold in any of these areas, stop. Avoid working at dusk, when the fading light can make pruning much more dangerous. No amount of experience qualifies you to work high up in a tree or ladder without proper safety equipment and a helper. Never work anywhere near power lines.

Pole Pruners. These feature either a pruning-saw blade or bypass pruners, or both, at the end of a wood or fiberglass pole that may or may not extend. They're useful for making overhead cuts, and it's safer to use them than to climb a ladder with loppers or a saw. Models with a fiberglass pole are lighter in weight and easier to control, especially when fully extended.

Pocket Knife. A sharp pocket knife is useful for heading back new growth that's too thick to pinch out with your fingers. You can also use a knife to remove soft, new growth such as water sprouts. Conventional pruning shears work just as well for this purpose, but a knife can be tucked into a back pocket, where it's always at hand. Look for a pruning knife, which has a blade that curves in slightly.

Gloves and Glasses. Never start a pruning operation without donning a pair of sturdy leather gloves and protective eyewear — sunglasses or prescription glasses at a minimum, true safety glasses for the best protection. Pruning involves sharp blades, pointed twigs, and flying bits of wood, all of which can result in accidents. Using basic safety equipment can prevent such problems.

BASIC TOOL CARE

Clean all your pruning tools after using them. If you are working with diseased plants, disinfect the tools with a solution of one part bleach to nine parts water (some experts recommend using straight bleach) or 70 percent alcohol. If your tools are not rustproof, rub on a light protective coating of oil before storing them. Tools with moving parts, such as pruning shears, need lubrication and occasional tightening and adjustment. Keep all cutting edges properly sharpened; each type of blade requires a different kind of edge, so unless you learn to sharpen your own tools and acquire the necessary jigs to do so, you should have a professional do it for you.

ing and know how to make the basic types of pruning cuts, you can use your knowledge and observation skills to reason your way to a solution.

Before you make the first cut, think about why you are pruning — to remove deadwood, to thin out dense, tangled stems, or to increase flowering, for example. Then examine the plant carefully to decide how best to accomplish your purpose; decide what cuts to make and review in your mind how they will affect the plant's growth. You can also refer to "A Guide to Pruning Flowering Trees, Shrubs, and Vines" on page 54 for tips on pruning particular species. Then take a deep breath and begin to cut.

As you work, step back and walk around the plant frequently to observe the results of your cuts. Consider the overall balance of the branching: shrubs should have well-spaced branches radiating in all directions, with no congested or lopsided growth. All sides of a tree should be equally dense, with no scaffold branch growing much more or much less vigorously than the others. If one branch seems to be outrunning the rest, head it back to an outward-facing bud not far from its growing tip to direct the growth into branching. To improve your pruning skills, observe your plants over the months and years to see how they grow both before and after pruning.

If you're really baffled or worried about damaging a plant, ask a knowledgeable friend or hire a reputable arborist to prune it for you. Watch him or her carefully and ask questions. A short "apprenticeship" like this can be invaluable.

TIPS FOR SUCCESS

LOOK AND LEARN BEFORE YOU CUT

If you are not sure how best to prune a woody plant, before you start to cut, study well-maintained examples of the plant in your neighborhood or at an arboretum or botanical garden. You'll be able to see what shape is most natural and whether the plant adapts well to a technique like shearing. You might also look at poorly pruned examples to figure out what mistakes to avoid.

Other excellent ways to learn are by asking experienced pruners for advice, attending a pruning demonstration, or taking a pruning workshop at your local arboretum, botanical garden, or garden center.

In this chapter, you'll find separate sections on how to prune trees, shrubs, and vines. Since not all plants are easily defined as one or the other, this system is somewhat arbitrary. What you consider to be a large shrub may be a small tree to someone else. Certain plants may be grown as perennials in the north, where they are killed to the ground each year, but as shrubs in the south.

For the most part, however, the distinction is fairly clear, and it is a useful one for discussing pruning practices. You should decide which classification

applies to your plant and prune accordingly. Shrubs are erect, self-supporting, multiple-stemmed woody plants that generally do not grow taller than about 12 or 15 feet. Trees tend to be taller than shrubs under normal conditions and generally develop a single stem, although multistemmed clumps of some trees, such as birches, are popular. Vines generally grow very fast, producing somewhat limp stems that need external support from a trellis or other structure or a surface on which to cling.

REDUCING PRUNING CHORES

Good pruning makes landscape plants more attractive, and it can also reduce long-term maintenance. Early pruning and training will help all woody plants develop the form best suited to the style you want, whether it be a sheared hedge or a naturally shaped tree or shrub. Early training pays dividends in the form of attractive, healthy plants that require minimal future shaping. Keep in mind, though, that the style of pruning you choose will greatly affect the amount of long-term maintenance required. Sheared hedges and foundation plants require attention several times a year — year after year — to look their best. Plants that are allowed to grow more naturally may require nothing more than occasional thinning to remove congested stems or heading back to shorten wayward branches or induce more flowers.

Your choice of plants can also make a major difference in your pruning chores. When carefully chosen to match the conditions and size of their site, many woody plants will thrive and look good with minimal attention. This is especially true if you allow your trees, shrubs, and vines to keep their natural forms. Then all you have to do with most of them is remove dead or damaged growth and unwanted suckers and thin misplaced, wayward, congested, and weak growth as needed throughout the year. With flowering shrubs you also may occasionally want to head back branches lightly after blooming to keep the shrub compact and encourage more flowers.

Plants that require constant pruning to reduce their size are in the wrong place; they should be removed and replaced. Not only will you reduce maintenance chores, but plants that need constant hacking back to keep them "in bounds" are rarely very attractive.

When choosing a replacement, carefully consider plant size *at maturity* before you buy. (You should find this information on the plant tag or in the catalog description. If you don't, and nursery personnel can't tell you the plant's size at maturity, shop elsewhere.) If you need a tree to plant under electrical wires, look for one recommended for this purpose. Planting an oak tree under wires is asking for never-ending pruning chores and frustration, while a small crab apple in the same site will provide years of pleasure with minimal work. Similarly, if you want low-growing shrubs around a foundation or under a window, select dwarf cultivars. For example, American arborvitae *(Thuja occidentalis)* looks cute and manageable in its pot at the nursery, but it matures at a stately 60 feet. Instead of spending your time wrestling with a full-size specimen, select one of the many cultivars available that won't exceed 3 feet. Dwarf or low-growing cultivars of most common evergreen foundation shrubs are available. By choosing them you will eliminate long-term pruning headaches and free up your time for more enjoyable pursuits, like playing golf or growing flowers.

Prune Trees Safely

Use a pole saw to reach lower branches of shade trees instead of climbing the tree or pruning from a ladder. Always make a three-step cut on large branches. Otherwise the branch can fall when cut partway through, tearing bark down the side of the tree.

PRUNING TREES

The stems, branches, and buds of both trees and shrubs respond to pruning in much the same way. Thinning cuts and heading cuts have similar effects. Trees, like shrubs, can be maintained with minimal pruning, mainly by promptly removing dead, damaged, or diseased wood.

Size, however, is an important difference. You can prune most shrubs while standing firmly on the ground, and cuts seldom require anything larger than pruning shears, loppers, or a small pruning saw. Furthermore, the severed stems and branches are almost never heavy enough to knock you off balance when they fall or to strain your back when you drag them away. Pruning any tree but a young or small one can be

a dangerous business, however. It's easy to see that training and experience are essential when the task is to remove a 300-pound, 10-inch-diameter branch growing 30 feet off the ground. But simpler jobs can be dangerous, too. It's surprisingly easy to tumble off the top of a stepladder, jarred by the sudden release of the 3-inch-thick branch you were sawing off. Broken bones are bad enough; imagine the outcome if you were perched on a ladder wielding a chain saw.

So for safety reasons alone, hire a professional arborist to do any tree pruning you can't accomplish while standing firmly on the ground using pruners, a hand pruning saw, or a pole saw. See "Choosing an Arborist" on page 33 for tips on finding the right person to prune your trees and shrubs.

Given this restriction, you can still do a fair amount of pruning on smaller mature trees. And with just a few simple techniques, you can help give young trees a good start toward an attractive shape and a long life of minimal pruning.

WHEN TO PRUNE TREES

According to an old expert's adage, the correct time to prune is whenever you have the saw in your hand. That holds true for dead or diseased branches, water sprouts, and suckers, which should be removed any time you notice them. For most other types of pruning, correct timing will help you achieve the best results.

Removing Suckers

Remove suckers that appear around the base of a tree or shrub at any time of year. Either pull them up or cut them at or below ground level.

In general, most trees respond best to pruning from late winter to very early spring. At that time of year the plants are still dormant, and wounds will heal very quickly once the plant begins growing in spring. Another advantage is that with deciduous trees, it's easy to see the branching structure before the leaves appear. If you don't get your pruning done by very early spring, put it off until summer, though. From the time the buds break in the spring through early summer, bark is very loose and easily torn. Pruning when a tree is actively growing in spring or early summer retards growth and slows wound closure because it removes carbohydrate energy. (For this reason, you can slow the growth of an

Understanding Wound Closure

Untended trees naturally shed their lower limbs as they grow. The limb detaches at the branch collar (the swelling where it attaches to the trunk), and a callus then forms over the wound. The wound closure is commonly, but misleadingly, referred to as healing. Damaged wood does not actually heal or regenerate; the tree simply concentrates metabolic chemical preservatives around the wound to isolate it.

Try to imitate this natural shedding and closure process when you are pruning. By cutting along the line just outside the branch collar, where the branch would naturally drop, you allow the tree to use its inherent closure and decay-resistance mechanisms most effectively. Even if a pruning wound becomes infected before it closes, the tree's chemical defenses will contain the infection, provided the tree is healthy and the wound has not breached the branch collar. In the first year after pruning, the layer of wood that forms is extremely resistant to penetration of decay from within, and the wound will be self-limiting unless that layer is subsequently wounded again. If a tree does develop a cavity, leave the repair to an expert. Or you can ignore it completely; a hollow but vigorous tree, left alone, can become stronger each year as the cavity is contained and the cambium continues to add layers to the sapwood.

The value of tree-wound dressings has been debated for decades. Many of the substances used to coat tree wounds do more harm than good, and they are seldom necessary. Some of the newer dressings that contain maleic hydrazide, naphthalene acetic acid, or chloro-fluorenol growth inhibitors in an asphalt emulsion, however, help prevent the growth of water sprouts and suckers where such problems are likely. Be sure to read the package directions before using such preparations so as not to affect wound closure and the growth of the tree.

overly vigorous tree by pruning in early summer, which is also a good time to remove water sprouts and suckers.)

Maples, elms, walnuts, birches, and some other trees will "bleed" if cut when the sap is rising in late winter and early spring. Although the loss of sap doesn't hurt the tree, the oozing can invite unsightly bacterial infections and sooty molds. You might defer heavy pruning of these species until midsummer, when new growth is hardened off. You can also prune in early winter, after the leaves have fallen and the tree is dormant. Oaks pruned in May or June are more liable to become infected with oak wilt, a fatal disease.

Avoid pruning in late summer or fall, because wound closure will not occur until the following spring, exposing the tree to winter damage. In addition, late-summer pruning may induce succulent new growth, which may not harden sufficiently before cold weather sets in, resulting in winter injury.

It is fine to prune in winter after trees are dormant, although they become increasingly brittle and are more easily damaged if they are pruned during extremely cold weather — below about 22 degrees F. Keep in mind that the onset of a severe cold snap within a few days of a winter pruning job can cause the freshly cut cambium to die back, enlarging the wounds, so watch the weather report before you decide to prune.

TRAINING YOUNG TREES

Young trees benefit immensely from early pruning and training. Not only does early pruning ensure a sound structure and attractive form, it will also eliminate or reduce the need for pruning at maturity, when the task becomes much more difficult. It's relatively easy, for example, to widen a narrow crotch or to remove a crossing branch on a young tree. You can also prune young trees simply for aesthetic reasons. By selectively thinning, pinching, and heading back, for instance, you can create an open form that will display attractive bark, flowers, or fruit to best advantage. Before you begin training a young tree, learn about the natural shape of the species or cultivar so you can work with that shape and train it accordingly.

When you plant a new tree, it is generally best not to prune until the second season, because too much pruning can inhibit growth. Remove broken or

oak *(Q. alba),* and many pines and firs bear branches that stick out at 90-degree angles from the trunk, while pin oak *(Q. palustris),* shingle oak *(Q. imbricaria),* and some spruces (*Picea* spp.) have descending branches. You'll rarely have to widen branch angles on these species. A few species are especially prone to producing narrow branch angles, including elms (*Ulmus* spp.), 'Bradford' pears (*Pyrus calleryana* 'Bradford'), American yellowwood *(Cladrastis lutea),* Japanese zelkova *(Zelkova serrata),* and poplars (*Populus* spp.).

On a young tree with slender branches it's easy to widen a narrow crotch with a simple spacer. Cut a light stick or piece of wooden lath to size, notch each end, and insert it between the branch and the trunk or the collar of a higher branch. Be careful not to force a branch too far all at once and split the crotch. Leave the spacer in place only during the growing season to minimize abrasions to the bark. You can also widen the angle of a crotch or otherwise direct the growth of a branch by tying it to the stakes supporting the young tree or even into the ground directly below the branch.

Eliminate Double Leaders. Many of our most prized landscape trees — ash, oak, pine, and spruce — have a characteristic columnar or pyramidal shape. The backbone of this shape is usually a single, strong trunk. But in some young trees the leading shoot forks, creating two competing leaders. If these both mature, the tree won't have its distinctive shape, and the resulting weak, narrow crotch may break under stress, leaving a disfigured specimen. On a conifer, you can simply trim the second leader off at its base. On other trees you can either remove the second leader entirely or cut it back to a bud about halfway along its length, forcing it to send out side shoots.

Replace Damaged or Missing Leaders. Occasionally weather, animals, or humans damage or destroy a young tree's leader. Fortunately, you can establish another leader simply by tying a healthy branch from below the point of damage to a vertical splint made of wood or bamboo. Attach the splint to the trunk and new leader with twine (if the trunk alone won't support it easily, tie the splint to a stout stake driven into the ground). Trim off the old leader just above the new one. Leave the splint in place until the new leader can support itself, which may take a year or two.

Replacing a Leader

To replace a leader that has been damaged or destroyed, train a branch to take its place by tying it to a splint that holds it upright. Use a stake if necessary to keep the splint vertical. Trim off the old, damaged leader.

Train Strong Scaffold Limbs. Ideally, the branches of a tree should form a spoke pattern out from the trunk, with about five branches to each wheel or tier of branches. For a large shade or ornamental tree, the optimum vertical distance between branches is 3 to 4 feet. Remove weak lateral branches on young trees annually to encourage growth of the main scaffold branches. Also thin out branches that stick out from the trunk at odd angles, point back into the center of the canopy, or rub or cross other branches. If two branches are growing too close together, especially if one is growing directly above the other, remove the weaker or less attractive one. If possible, try to anticipate problems and head them off before they occur: remove branches that will compete with the central leader and ones that will cross or rub if they continue growing unchecked, for example.

Young oaks, pines, flowering dogwoods, and some maples have a tendency to produced whorled branches, which means that multiple crotches develop where three or more limbs join. If you are thinning out a group of such limbs, some of which may be nearly as large as the trunk, don't cut adjacent limbs at the same time. Cut every second or third limb and temporarily head back the others. Then wait a year or two before removing the remainder. Doing this will allow the leader to recover dominance and will minimize the girdling effect that sometimes results from cutting the whole whorl at once.

Limb Up for Headroom. As the young tree grows, you'll have to decide whether you need headroom to walk beneath it or want its branches to sweep the ground. Evergreens are generally grown with their branches extending all the way to the ground. Most shade trees, on the other hand, are limbed up to provide room underneath for enjoyment of the shade. Limbing up also makes it easier to tend grass or grow groundcovers or perennials under a shade tree. Deciduous trees that naturally produce descending branches, including pin oak and shingle oak, often look awkward when limbed up; plant these species away from walkways and let the branches sweep the ground for a natural effect and low maintenance.

If you decide to limb up a tree, do not remove the lower branches for the first few years after planting. It has been shown that these branches help the tree develop a thicker trunk. Beginning in about the fourth year of growth, remove the lowest branches at the same rate that new branches are being formed at the tree's top. Work up from the bottom over a two- or three-year period. A good plan is to cut back each of the lowest side branches by about one-third (to a point where a smaller side branch joins it) the first year; the next year, remove those pruned branches entirely and head back the next tier of branches by one-third. Continue this process for several years until the lowest branches are growing at the desired height.

PRUNING MATURE TREES

If you've purchased a well-formed young tree and pruned it judiciously, you'll have little pruning to do when it's mature. This is particularly true of conifers such as pine, firs, and spruces. Leave the rejuvenation of neglected mature trees

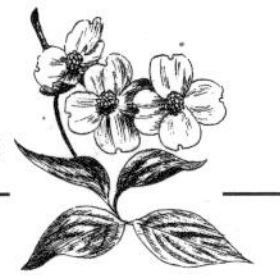

Choosing an Arborist

Mature trees not only contribute to the dollar value of your property, they add unquestionable appeal to the landscape; you shouldn't entrust their maintenance to just any run-of-the-mill tree service. Don't hire an unqualified tree trimmer, who may leave you with a hacked-up, ruined tree that is also open to disease and insect infestation. Good arborists don't have to canvass neighborhoods door to door to find clients. Avoid companies that won't provide an estimate or that offer their services at unbelievably cheap prices, try to push you into removing a live tree, or suggest topping your trees or rounding off their tops.

Instead, get recommendations from other homeowners or find an arborist certified by the International Society of Arboriculture (write or call ISA, P.O. Box GG, Savoy, IL 61874, (217) 355-9411 for a local recommendation). Neighbors or a local arboretum or botanic garden are also good sources. Ask for references and don't be shy about asking to see your arborist's previous pruning jobs. It is also a good idea to ask for proof of insurance coverage, including workers' compensation and personal and property damage coverage. Finally, if everything seems in order, stand back and let the expert do the job.

and treatment of disease to a certified arborist — as well as any other pruning above a height you can comfortably reach from the ground. Climbing into a tree without a safety harness, especially if the tree is decayed or otherwise hazardous, is dangerous, as is climbing up a ladder with sharp tools. *Never* work around trees or shrubs that are near power lines or extend over traffic.

Removing Water Sprouts and Suckers. Water sprouts on lower branches can easily be trimmed off at their base with pruning shears or loppers. Suckers, which are vigorous vertical shoots that appear around the base of the trunk or from the roots of some trees, are easy to dispatch as well. On grafted plants some suckers may sprout from below the graft union, and in some species lawnmower damage to surface roots also produces suckers. Other plants produce suckers naturally as a means of spreading or propagating themselves, including sumacs, sassafras, some plum trees, and aspens. Such trees naturally grow in clumps or groves.

Removing suckers regularly will help keep your garden tidy, although gardeners who enjoy a less tame-looking landscape may prefer to let the suckers of clump-forming species grow. Suckers are less likely to grow back if you pull, rather than cut, them, preferably during their first growing season. After cutting off older, woody suckers, try treating the wound with a growth inhibitor to discourage the production of more suckers. Using mulch to shade and protect the roots can also be helpful. Regardless of the growing environment you provide, plants that survive by root suckering will send up occasional sprouts.

Removing Limbs. You can remove older limbs that are damaged or dead, provided you can reach them with a pruning saw or a pole saw. You may also want to remove branches that interfere with a view of the garden or block a walkway.

Limbing Up a Tree

If a tree is blocking traffic, remove one or two of the lower branches annually. Pin oaks and other trees with naturally descending branches are best planted away from sidewalks, paths, and driveways.

Whenever you are removing a healthy branch, it's best to begin by heading it back at least a year in advance. This retards the diameter growth of the limb, meaning that its diameter will be less than the diameter of the parent limb or trunk. The ratio between these diameters governs the speed at which a pruning wound closes. As long as the size and rate of growth of the parent limb or trunk significantly exceed the size and rate of growth of the limb, the eventual final pruning cut should close quickly.

When removing a large branch, always use a three-step cut, as shown on page 7; otherwise the weight of the branch may tear it loose from the tree before you've completed the cut. Take care to position the final cut so you don't injure the branch collar. Avoid using a chain saw for pruning, because it can be hard to control. Unless you are an expert, it's hard to make clean, proper pruning cuts with a chain saw. *Never* make a cut with a chain saw that requires you to hold the saw higher than chest level.

You may want simply to shorten a branch that has grown too long, giving the tree an unbalanced look. Figure out how much of the limb to remove to restore the tree's visual equilibrium, then make the cut just above the nearest side shoot that grows in a direction you prefer. If the portion you're removing is large or heavy, cut it back in several stages. (Remember that most pines and some other conifers won't sprout new growth from old wood.)

PRUNING TECHNIQUES FOR PROFESSIONALS

A professional arborist can perform a variety of pruning tasks on even very large trees that will make them healthier, safer, and more attractive. Use the list below as well as the illustration on page 37 as a guide to the kinds of services an arborist can perform and problems he or she can correct.

Correcting Narrow Crotches. A narrow crotch with embedded or included bark generally will become weaker and more subject to splitting as the tree grows. Narrow branches that arise near the top of a tree may begin to compete with the central leader, forming a double trunk of sorts. An arborist can remove weak growth or can brace or cable branches that might break off under stress.

Crown Thinning and Reduction. An expert can reduce the size of a tree's crown without destroying its natural shape. If you must reduce the height or crown weight of a tree, an arborist can combine a technique called drop-crotch pruning with selective thinning. For a drop-crotch cut, he or she cuts back the branch to where it meets a branch that is smaller but not less than about one-third the size of the first branch. Thinning cuts will remove excess growth and open up the center of the tree to light and air.

TIPS FOR SUCCESS

JUST SAY NO TO TOPPING!

This so-called pruning method involves cutting off most of the crown by sawing off branches without regard to the tree's natural shape. Avoid topping at all costs, along with any tree service that recommends it. The result is a disfigured tree with a canopy of stumps (somewhat umbrella-shaped) that sprout dense clumps of weak shoots. These shoots need constant pruning to keep them in bounds. The process is extremely stressful for the tree and leaves it open to disease and insect infestations. Topping, sometimes called dehorning, is often the method used to cope with too-large trees growing under power lines, but topped trees are seldom worth having; replacement is generally the best option.

Stormproofing. Stormproofing combines a variety of techniques, including crown thinning and reduction as well as cabling and bracing, to make a tree safer in a windstorm. Along with removing weak growth and thinning branches to reduce wind resistance, the goal is to reduce the weight of the crown and shape it so that if the tree falls, it will fall away from the house or other buildings. For valuable specimens or trees on high ground, an arborist can also install cables that ground the tree and minimize lightning damage.

Storm Repair. An arborist will be able to tell you whether a tree damaged in a storm can be pruned to remove broken, damaged growth or should be removed entirely.

Disease Control. Pruning can control certain diseases, but fast action is necessary. For example, localized fire blight, oak wilt, or Dutch elm disease can sometimes be stopped by pruning off a branch before the fungus spreads. The final cut should be made with a sterilized saw at least 10 feet closer to the roots than the last sign of leaf wilt or of discoloration of the phloem, or sapwood. If the infection is systemic, pruning will not help, but you might be able to isolate the disease from susceptible trees nearby by removing the infected tree and then cutting the roots, midway between the trees, to a depth of at least 3 feet to remove root grafts that may have occurred between them. Be sure to burn or dispose of all infected trimmings.

Pruning Mature Trees

Mature trees that were not trained at an early age may have a variety of problems, such as those shown here, that can be corrected by an arborist. Specimens that were pruned and trained early generally need only occasional attention.

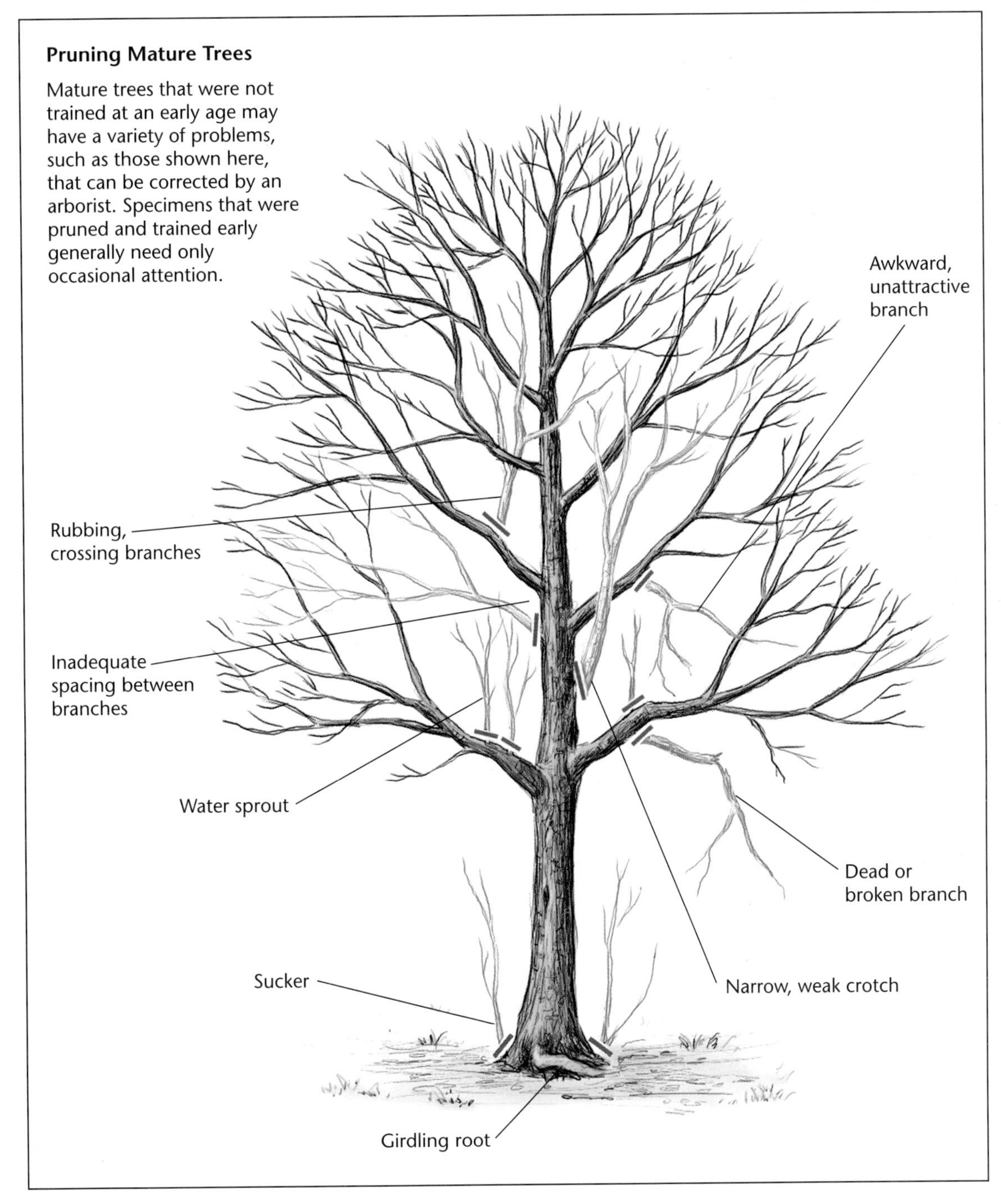

Tree Removal. Taking down a large tree for any reason is a job for a professional. A certified arborist can remove a tree with minimal damage to your landscape — and none to your house.

PRUNING SHRUBS

Although shrubs come in a staggering array of shapes and sizes, they are simpler to prune than you might think. The first step is knowing how to make proper heading and thinning cuts and understanding how plants will respond to each type of cut. When you combine this knowledge with clear pruning goals and information about the specific plant — its form or habit, whether it blooms on old wood or new, and its age, for example — you'll be well on your way to approaching nearly any pruning chore with confidence. Use the considerations below to guide you, and see "A Guide to Pruning Flowering Trees, Shrubs, and Vines" on page 54 for recommendations on various species.

TIPS FOR SUCCESS

PLAN YOUR PRUNING

If you are tackling a shrub or vine with a confusing array of congested growth, try marking branches for removal with ribbon or yarn before you start. That way you can plan your cuts in advance and you'll be less likely to remove a branch accidentally. Even with marked branches, it's useful to step back from the plant frequently to evaluate the plant's shape.

Consider Form. Learn about the natural habit of a shrub before you decide how to prune it. Some shrubs look best when thinned and allowed to assume a natural shape, while others are suitable for shearing. Common lilac (*Syringa* spp.), with its heavy, upright branches, would look stubby if sheared, for example, but lilacs can be shaped and kept vigorous by annual thinning out of the oldest stems. Forsythia is another shrub that should not be sheared; plants cut into globes or other sheared shapes always have fewer flowers than specimens allowed to assume their natural, arching shape. On the other hand, compact, twiggy shrubs with dense habits of growth and small leaves, like privets and boxwood, adapt well to shearing.

Consider Age and Vigor. A vigorous young shrub will respond to pruning in a different manner than an older, slower-growing one. Consider this difference in deciding how radically to prune a plant. For example, the general prescription for a shrub that is no longer producing flowers is to prune out older wood and

allow new growth to spring up. You may even be able to cut a young shrub to the ground to induce new flowering wood, although not all species will tolerate this practice. For an older plant that's producing only one or two new branches or canes each year, thinning out one or more of the oldest branches annually may be the best approach.

Consider the Landscape Use. Choose your pruning style according to the shrub's specific site or use in the landscape. Pruning can highlight the natural shape and maximize bloom on shrubs used as specimens or growing in a shrub border. Heading cuts will encourage dense branching on shrubs intended to block unsightly views. Use thinning cuts to encourage a graceful, open habit or to control size. Formal hedges must be sheared, but a more natural hedge can be pruned with heading and thinning cuts.

Effective Shrub Shaping

Most shrubs can be maintained with a combination of thinning and heading cuts. First step back and visualize the shape you would like the shrub to have.

Start by removing deadwood, then thin out old wood, as well as crossing, rubbing, or crowded branches. Use heading cuts to shorten growth that is too long and to encourage branching.

Determining Pruning Style

The pruning style you select can depend as much on the landscape situation as the plant itself. Here a yew has been pruned three different ways for three different purposes.

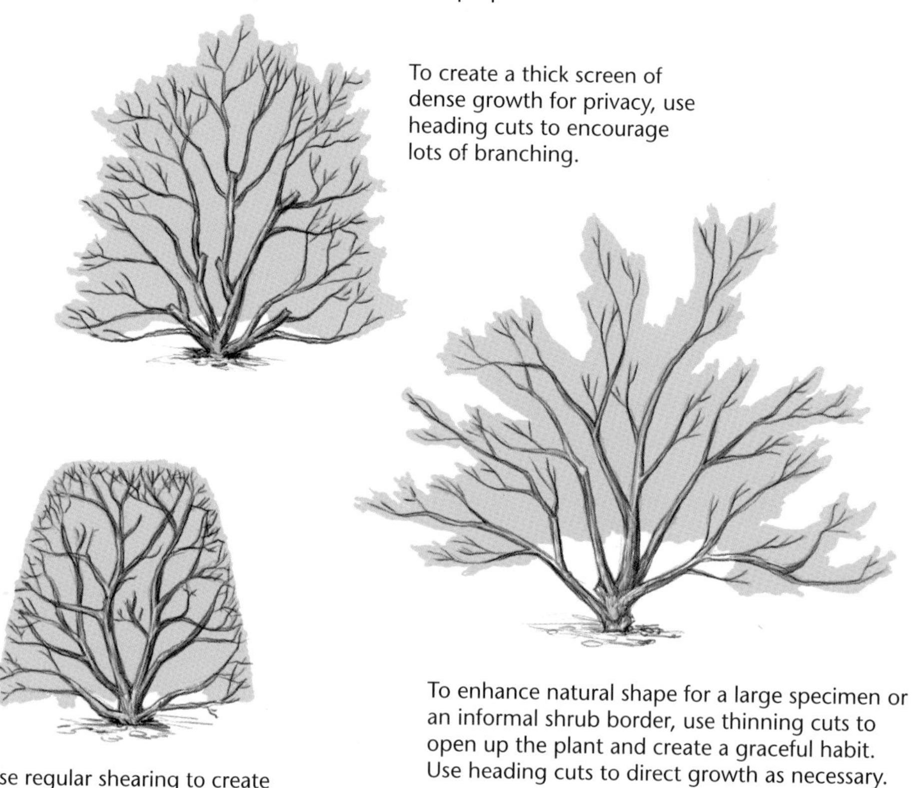

To create a thick screen of dense growth for privacy, use heading cuts to encourage lots of branching.

To enhance natural shape for a large specimen or an informal shrub border, use thinning cuts to open up the plant and create a graceful habit. Use heading cuts to direct growth as necessary.

Use regular shearing to create a formal hedge.

Consider the Plant's Features. Whether or not a plant is grown for its flowers obviously affects the type of pruning you do as well as its timing. Some shrubs, such as pyracanthas and some viburnums, are grown for their showy fruit as well as their flowers. Shearing or deadheading them will reduce or eliminate the fruit display. Thinning lightly immediately after flowering is usually best for retaining fruit and promoting next year's bloom. Shrubs with especially colorful young stems or new foliage are pruned for aesthetic reasons alone. For example, red-osier dogwood *(Cornus sericea)* has attractive red or yellow stems, and if the plants

are cut to the ground in winter, new, more brightly colored branches will replace the old. In some cultivars of smoke tree *(Cotinus coggygria)* the new foliage is bright purple. Annual spring pruning sacrifices summer flowers but ensures a showy foliage display.

You also may need to prune to remove reverted growth, such as branches with all green leaves on a plant that is supposed to be variegated. Dwarf plants, especially conifers, sometimes produce branches that revert to the normal speed of growth of the nondwarf form. These branches will overwhelm the plant if they are not thinned out.

When to Prune Shrubs

Remove dead, damaged, or diseased wood as well as suckers and water sprouts at any time of year. If flowering is not a consideration, pruning deciduous shrubs in late winter or very early spring is often easiest because the branch structure is easy to see. See "A Guide to Pruning Flowering Trees, Shrubs, and Vines" on page 54 for specific recommendations.

Pruning Flowering Shrubs. For shrubs grown for their flowers or showy berries, the best time to prune healthy wood depends mainly on whether blooms are produced on new wood — that is, the current season's growth — or on old wood, formed the previous year. (Keep in mind that you can prune any flowering shrub in late winter or early spring, regardless of what wood it blooms on; you simply may sacrifice some of the bloom for a season.)

In general, spring-flowering plants, such as lilacs, flowering quinces, and forsythias, bloom on old wood. Prune them shortly after they've flowered so they can form new buds for next year's display. Pruning in fall, late winter, or early spring will cut off most of the bud wood and the shrub will bloom sparsely, if at all.

Plants that bloom later, such as potentillas, hypericums, and beautyberries (*Callicarpa* spp.) usually do so on new wood. Prune them in late fall after the plants are dormant or in winter or very early spring. New flowering wood will develop during that growing season. Also prune plants that bloom twice or throughout the growing season in late winter.

PRUNING TECHNIQUES FOR SHRUBS

For most shrubs, pruning is simply a matter of making a series of heading and thinning cuts to enhance shape, performance, and plant vigor. See "Types of Pruning Cuts" on page 4 for more information on how to make these cuts and how they affect plant growth.

Heading Back. You head back a shrub by making a series of cuts across stems just above a bud. Heading cuts will induce branching and can be used to promote dense, twiggy growth as well as promote flowering. Always cut back to a bud facing in a direction you want the new growth to take (usually away from the center of the shrub). Pinching or cutting off growing tips is also a form of heading back that induces branching and encourages compact growth in shrubs, just as it does in herbaceous plants.

Since heading cuts induce growth, avoid them if you are trying to control the size of a plant; thinning cuts are more effective for this purpose.

> **TIPS FOR SUCCESS**
>
> **DEADHEADING SHRUBS**
>
> Removing the spent flowers on shrubs will improve their appearance and make available to roots and shoots energy that would otherwise be used to set seed or fruit. Remove only the spent flowers, taking care not to cut any buds at the base. Deadheading will not stimulate reblooming of most shrubs, and it isn't practical on large shrubs or those that do not bear their flowers in large clusters. Also, don't deadhead shrubs that bear decorative fruits.

Thinning. Thinning cuts are used to remove the weakest or oldest growth, cut out dead and diseased wood, eliminate crossing and rubbing branches, and open up crowded portions of a shrub to light and air. Canes or stems that arise from a crown can be cut back to the ground. Treelike woody shrubs can be thinned by removing the unwanted branches back to a crotch. Be sure to cut just outside the branch collar, and don't leave a stub, which invites disease — if you can hang your hat on the stub, it's too long. Use pruning shears or loppers, or a saw if the branches are thick. Thinning cuts are the best way to remove water sprouts and reverted growth. Suckers are less likely to grow back if pulled; if that is impossible, remove them with thinning cuts.

Rejuvenation. Rejuvenation, sometimes called renovation or renewal pruning, is a thinning process that promotes new growth and increases vigor by replacing old wood with new growth. It can be done radically or gradually, but it is not

Thinning Shrubs

Removing entire stems, canes, or branches can improve the appearance and health of a shrub.

Where numerous stems sprout from a crown, cut some back to the ground.

For shrubs with just a few stems or trunks, thin by cutting branches back to a crotch. Avoid leaving stubs.

suitable for every type of shrub. Only plants that sprout readily from old wood are capable of initiating new growth after radical pruning. If you aren't sure whether a given plant will withstand rejuvenation, it's best to ask at a nursery. Or look among the older stems for suckers, which are a good indication that it will resprout. For example, an old neglected lilac that looks like a cloud of suckers surrounding a maze of old, diseased, and dead stems is an excellent candidate for rejuvenation.

For radical rejuvenation, simply cut the entire shrub to within a few inches of the ground in late winter or early spring, using pruning shears or loppers for small stems and a saw for larger ones. Some aged or crowded shrubs may not require or respond well to such drastic treatment and should be cut to 2 feet or more above the ground; cotoneasters, privets, and lilacs can be rejuvenated in this way. Suckering plants can be rejuvenated by removing the old growth and encouraging selected suckers. If a shrub is healthy and has adequate energy reserves, it will respond to rejuvenation with vigorous juvenile growth that can be worked into a shapely, manageable specimen with subsequent annual prun-

Shrub Makeovers

One way to deal with a large, overgrown shrub is to transform it into a small tree. You can select a single trunk and prune away all other growth or create a multistemmed specimen, as shown here. Either way, prune the plant gradually to keep it healthy and vigorous.

Step 1. Select the thickest stems to become the trunks of the new tree. An odd number of trunks is generally most attractive. Remove suckers and smaller stems around the new trunks.

Step 2. Limb up the new trunks by cutting off the lower branches over the course of two or three years.

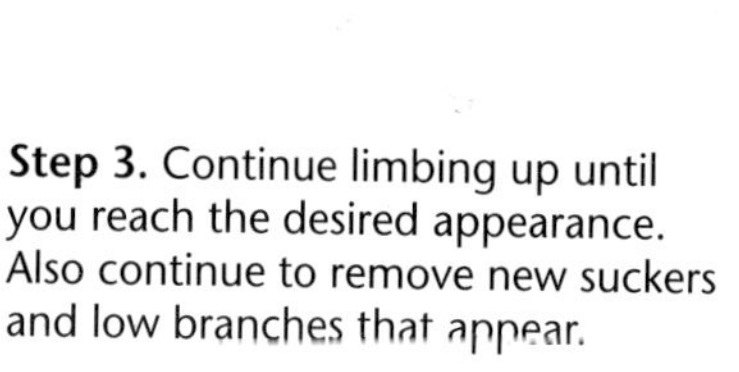

Step 3. Continue limbing up until you reach the desired appearance. Also continue to remove new suckers and low branches that appear.

Rejuvenating Shrubs

Some shrubs look their best when cut back to the ground either annually or every few years.

Some shrubs, such as lilacs, respond to rejuvenation best if a portion of the old wood is retained. Cut most of the stems back to ground level; retain some old growth, cut to between 2 and 6 feet in height, as well as a few younger suckers to form new stems.

ing. Shrubs that sprout readily from old wood, such as forsythias, willows, spireas, old-fashioned weigela *(Weigela florida),* and beautybush (*Kolkwitzia* spp.) can be rejuvenated annually or maintained by more subtle combinations of thinning and heading back; your choice will depend on the effect you desire and on the ornamental value of the stems, juvenile bark, and flowers.

In clump-forming plants, it is often a good idea to reduce the diameter of the clump by severing its peripheral suckers and then pulling them up from

Gradual Rejuvenation

Follow the steps below annually to rejuvenate an older shrub over the course of two or three years.

Step 1. Remove any deadwood, then cut two or three of the oldest stems to within 2 or 3 inches of the ground.

Step 2. Use thinning cuts to remove crossing or rubbing stems and those that ruin the plant's shape.

Step 3. Cut back remaining stems by one-half to encourage vigorous new growth. Remove excess twiggy growth. Cut above a bud or to a branch that points to the outside of the plant.

underground. To do this, use a sharp spade to cut a circle around the core of the plant; hold the spade nearly horizontal as you slice downward so that you cut through the suckers rather than merely pushing them farther underground.

Many shrubs that are hardy in the south die back to the ground each winter in the north. These "dieback" shrubs, which bear attractive flowers or bark on new growth, include bluebeard (*Caryopteris* spp.), butterfly bush (*Buddleia* spp.), chaste tree (*Vitex* spp.), and Russian sage *(Perovskia atriplicifolia).* Rejuvenate them by cutting them to the ground late each fall or in early spring prior to bud break, as you would for herbaceous perennials.

If you are concerned that the total removal of all growth may be too much of a shock (for the plant or for yourself), rejuvenate gradually. Remove a portion of the oldest stems or canes each year for two or three years. You can remove up to one-third of the oldest stems on vigorous plants; remove only a stem or two on less vigorous specimens. Once a rejuvenated shrub has begun to thrive again, continue thinning out a few of the oldest stems annually to keep it growing and looking its best.

Shearing. Formal hedges, some specimen shrubs (often those in foundation plantings), and topiary are pruned and trained to a specific outline or shape, then maintained by shearing. When you shear, you make no attempt to cut each shoot

Correct Shearing Shapes

Whether you are shearing a formal hedge or a foundation plant, make sure that the base remains wider than the top. Otherwise light will not reach the bottom of the plant, and growth will be spindly and sparse at the bottom.

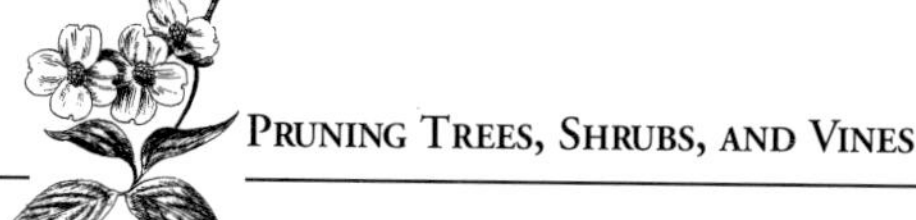

or branch near a bud, as you do in other forms of pruning. Instead, you cut with long-bladed hedge shears or an electrically powered hedge trimmer wherever necessary to create the desired flat or contoured surface. Properly tended, a sheared plant will remain vigorous through periods of controlled, almost unnoticeable growth.

Shearing can prove disastrous if performed on the wrong plants. Some plants, such as privets (*Ligustrum* spp.) and boxwoods (*Buxus* spp.), can recover from even the most radical shearing and form a respectable hedge or foundation plant. Other, more open shrubs, such as forsythia, will survive the ordeal but will look terrible. They're best used in a natural hedge or shrub border. Flowering shrubs such as rhododendrons and azaleas, weigela, and mock orange (*Philadelphus* spp.) also are not appropriate for formal hedges or other such uses, because shearing will remove their flowers. They can be used in informal, unsheared shrub borders, however.

PRUNING HEDGES

The proper treatment for a hedge depends on whether it is formal or informal. Formal hedges are clipped into rounded or squared-off shapes and require frequent shearing; informal hedges are maintained with heading cuts and occasional thinning cuts to encourage dense growth yet maintain the shrub's natural shape. In both styles the hedge should be several inches wider at the bottom than at the top so that the leaves on lower branches can receive sunlight. Otherwise, the lower branches will die, and it can be very difficult to induce them to resprout.

For formal hedges, choose shrubs with naturally dense, twiggy growth, small leaves, and inconspicuous flowers. Boxwood, euonymus, and privet are popular hedge plants. Conifers such as junipers and hemlocks also make attractive formal hedges.

A hedge that you plan to shear should be pruned a few weeks after planting and regularly thereafter. Head back newly planted hedge plants by one-third to one-half. (Don't head back most conifers.) After growth resumes, shear it back to a somewhat shortened, undersized version of the desired final shape. Be careful to establish a full base that is broader than the top. Allow the hedge to increase in size very slightly each year for several years, until a dense peripheral branch

Pruning Hedges

For best results, trim formal, sheared hedges frequently. If necessary, use strings along the top and/or sides of the hedge to provide a trimming guide.

structure has been developed. Clip the new growth lightly now and then throughout the spring and early summer. (You can use the same process to rejuvenate an overgrown hedge.)

When it comes to frequency of pruning, a hedge is similar to a lawn. You can clip it infrequently if you don't mind a rough, informal appearance. If you want a tidier look, you must clip it every three or four weeks during the summer or whenever you notice new growth of more than a couple of inches. In any case, the first clipping of the season should be done in late spring, after the new growth has matured. Cut back to the line of the hedge, the point where old growth becomes new. This forces the plant to send out side branches, filling in the hedge. Then shear as needed until the middle of summer. If you live in a cold climate, stop pruning at least six weeks before the first fall frost to allow subsequent growth to harden off before winter. To minimize sunscald on leaves and twigs, avoid heavy shearing during extremely hot, sunny periods.

PRUNING EVERGREENS

For the most part, you can prune evergreens in much the same way that you prune deciduous plants. There are, however, some specific guidelines to remember about pruning certain types of evergreens.

New growth can be pinched or headed back, if necessary, to induce more branching. Removing half or all of the tender new-growth "candles" of spruces (*Picea* spp.), firs (*Abies* spp.), and most pines (*Pinus* spp.) in late May or early June will force buds along the length or at the base of the candles into growth. (New growth is usually a lighter green than the old.) Likewise, you can pinch, shear, or head back the new growth of junipers (*Juniperus* spp.), arborvitae (*Thuja* spp.), hemlocks (*Tsuga* spp.), and certain other evergreens.

Be careful when heading back conifers into old wood, however. Some species will readily initiate new growth from old wood and others won't. When trimming yews (*Taxus* spp.), spruces, or firs, clip back to a pair of lateral buds to induce branching the next growing season. Yews also can be cut back to old wood, if necessary, because they will form adventitious buds. Junipers, arborvitae, pines, hemlocks, and certain other evergreens will not sprout dependably from old wood, so you should not head them back or shear them beyond the peripheral green zone of live foliage.

Some broad-leaved evergreens, such as bayberry and boxwood, will tolerate almost any pruning style. Prune rhododendrons and azaleas to enhance flowering as well as foliage by deadheading spent flowers (without damaging adjacent buds) and pinching the tips of new growth to increase bud set. Because rhododendrons are subject to root diseases, they should not be root pruned, but the suckers should be removed from below the bud union on grafted plants.

Conifers require almost no pruning, save for replacing a damaged leader or cutting out damaged branches or deadwood. Shearing can turn conifers into high-maintenance headaches. If you decide to shear, start when the tree is young to build up a dense branching structure, as described for a hedge on page 48. Once you begin to shear a conifer, you will have to continue the treatment annually, regardless of the tree's height. Otherwise, you will have to contend with a corona of loose growth around a dense core, which is not a pretty sight. A conifer's natural shape often is aesthetically superior to the smooth outline of a tightly sheared one, and it requires no annual follow-up.

Like flowering shrubs, vines may bloom on either old or new wood. Different varieties of clematis bloom on growth produced during the current season, on growth produced the previous year, or on both, so it is essential to know the type you have before you prune.

Pruning Vines

Like trees and shrubs, vines are pruned to remove deadwood and remove older growth that is no longer flowering to make room for more vigorous new shoots. They're also pruned to keep the flowers where you'll be able to see them. Since most vines flower on new wood, you'll want to prune them occasionally so the blooms aren't 60 feet up in the air. Many vines are pruned simply to keep them from taking over. Cut these rampant growers whenever and wherever they extend beyond their intended bounds. Root pruning may also help slow their growth.

Some vines grown for their attractive flowers, such as wisteria, can be pinched or headed back to encourage more flowers. During the winter you can cut wisteria shoots back to the second or third bud from their base. Clematis doesn't need pruning to increase the flowers, but you may want to thin out the shoots to make the plant look better. You'll find details on pruning popular vines in "A Guide to Pruning Flowering Trees, Shrubs, and Vines" on page 54. See Chapter 3 for details on pruning grapes.

Woody vines can be classified as clingers, twiners, tendril formers, or ramblers. The clingers, such as winter creeper *(Euonymus fortunei),* Boston ivy *(Partheno-*

Pruning Vines

To control the height and spread of vigorous vines, establish a basic framework of low branches. Then cut back to within one or two buds of the framework branches each year to encourage vigorous growth close to the ground. The time of pruning depends on whether the vine blooms on old or new wood.

cissus tricuspidata), and woodbine *(P. quinquefolia),* attach to their support by developing permanent specialized aerial roots. Twiners, such as morning glories (*Ipomoea* spp.), bittersweet (*Celastrus* spp.), wisteria (*Wisteria* spp.), and some honeysuckles (*Lonicera* spp.), wrap their stems around the support in a helical pattern. Some tendril formers, such as grapes, hold onto their support with twining leaf bracts; others, such as clematis, use twining leaf petioles. Ramblers, including brambles and climbing roses, simply grow fast, covering the ground or anything else they can lean upon and become entangled in. When pruning ornamental vines, keep these differences in mind. You'll have to pull down clingers and unwind twiners when you prune.

Espalier

Vines aren't the only plants that can be grown against a wall or trellis. Espalier is a technique used to train trees and shrubs in two dimensions, either against a wall or trellis or as free-standing specimens. Pyracanthas, crab apples, many fruit trees, and some evergreens, including Atlas cedar *(Cedrus atlantica),* lend themselves to this technique. Patterns can be as simple or complex as you like. See "Espalier" on page 81 for more information and directions for creating a Belgian fence.

Shrubs and small trees can be pruned and trained to cover a wall or fence using a technique called espalier. Because the plants are trained to grow in two dimensions, espalier is especially effective for adding height and color in a minimum of space.

A Guide to Pruning Flowering Trees, Shrubs, and Vines

Most shade trees, evergreens, and deciduous shrubs require minimal pruning in maturity. The following guide will help you prune woody plants that are grown for their flowers.

■ *Abelia* / Abelia

These summer-blooming shrubs produce flowers on the current season's growth. To encourage an abundance of flowers, remove winter-damaged growth and thin out approximately one-third of the oldest stems in late winter or early spring on established plants. Plants can be rejuvenated by cutting to within 3 inches of the ground.

■ *Actinidia* / Kiwi

Prune kiwi vines in winter to early spring to keep them in check. Or cut them back after flowering in early summer. The plants can also be trained in much the same way as grapes to maintain fruiting wood.

■ *Aristolochia* / Dutchman's Pipe

Prune these fast-growing vines heavily in winter or early spring to keep them in check. Or cut them back after flowering in early summer. Plants can be cut to the ground for renewal.

■ *Berberis* / Barberry

Thin out crowded growth in late winter or early spring by removing several of the oldest stems. Plants can also be pruned after they flower in spring. Wear gloves for protection against the thorny stems. Barberries make fine hedges, but avoid shearing them; they have an attractive natural shape.

■ *Buddleia* / Butterfly Bush

Fountain buddleia *(B. alternifolia)* blooms on the previous season's wood; prune it in summer immediately after it has finished blooming. Orange-eye butterfly bush *(B. davidii)* blooms on new wood. In northern zones, it may die to the ground in winter and can be treated as a herbaceous perennial. In areas where it is not killed back, prune one-third of the stems back to within 6 or 8 inches of

No-Prune Flowering Shrubs

The flowering shrubs listed below need almost no pruning, except for removing dead and damaged growth as well as crossing and rubbing branches. Bayberry *(Myrica pensylvanica)* can be pruned if necessary at any time of year. The other species bloom on old wood and should be pruned, if at all, immediately after they flower.

- *Daphne* spp. (daphnes)
- *Hamamelis* spp. (witch hazels)
- *Kalmia* spp. (mountain laurel)
- *Myrica pensylvanica* (bayberry)
- *Rhododendron* spp. (rhododendrons and azaleas)
- *Pieris* spp. (pieris)

the ground in late winter or early spring. Or rejuvenate the plant by cutting back all stems. Deadheading flowers as they fade will encourage bloom all summer long.

■ *Buxus* / Boxwood

These evergreens look attractive with minimal pruning. Remove winter-damaged growth and wayward stems that detract from the overall shape. Boxwoods can also be sheared, either annually in late winter or early spring for a more informal shape or periodically through the summer for a formal hedge. Plants will withstand rejuvenation pruning to within several inches of the ground, although it will take several years for them to recover.

■ *Callicarpa* / Beautyberry

These deciduous shrubs are grown for their clusters of tiny flowers in summer and small purple berries borne on new wood. Remove up to one-third of the oldest stems in late winter or early spring to keep plants vigorous. Beautyberries will withstand rejuvenation pruning; cut overgrown plants to within several inches of the ground in late winter or early spring if necessary.

▪ *Campsis* / Trumpet Vine

Also called trumpet creepers, these vigorous vines produce their flowers on new wood. Prune plants back to a few buds in late winter or early spring, if possible.

▪ *Chaenomeles* / Flowering Quince

Prune these shrubs after they bloom, since flowers appear on old wood. On mature specimens, remove two to three of the oldest, most crowded stems to open up the center of the plant. Plants can be rejuvenated by cutting back to within 2 to 3 inches of the ground.

▪ *Clematis* / Clematis

These spectacular vines can be confusing to prune because some bloom on new wood, others on old wood, and still others on both. There are three pruning regimes, based on bloom season and growth habit.

Clematis jackmanii and related cultivars bloom on new wood, generally in summer or fall. Prune them in late winter or early spring just before buds begin to swell. Cut them back to the lowest pair of strong buds annually; otherwise the flowers will be borne higher and higher on the plant each year. For a somewhat taller framework, cut back to 4 or 6 inches above the lowest pair of strong buds. Cultivars in this group include 'Crimson Star', 'Gipsy Queen', 'Hagley Hybrid', 'Mrs Cholmondeley', and 'Pearl of India'. Species include *C. orientalis, C. paniculata, C. tangutica, C. texensis,* and *C. viticella.* Cultivars with *C. viticella* parentage can also be pruned in this manner, including 'Duchess of Sutherland', 'Ernest Markham', 'Lady Betty Balfour', and 'Ville de Lyon'.

The second type of clematis produces flowers in spring on old wood and may produce a second flush of growth later in the season on new wood. Prune in late winter or early spring, before growth begins. Remove dead and damaged growth, and cut back to a strong pair of buds within 2 to 4 feet of the ground. Cultivars in this group include 'Candida', 'Elsa Späth', 'Lady Northcliffe', 'Ramona', 'Violet Charm', and 'William Kennett'. 'Beauty of Worcester' and 'Crimson King' produce double flowers on old wood and single flowers on new. 'Henryi', 'Lord Neville', and 'Nelly Moser' are especially free-flowering.

Cultivars derived from *C. patens,* as well as *C. florida,* flower on old wood.

Prune out dead and damaged growth in spring, then cut back several of the oldest shoots hard immediately after flowering. This encourages new growth, which will flower the following year. *C. patens* cultivars in this group include 'Barbara Jackman', 'Bees Jubilee', 'Lincoln Star', 'Marcel Moser', and 'The President'. *C. florida* cultivars include 'Belle of Woking', 'Duchess of Edinburgh', and 'Kathleen Dunford'.

▪ *Cornus* / Dogwood

Red-osier dogwood *(C. sericea)* is grown for its colorful red or yellow twigs. Since young wood is the most colorful, cut one-third of the oldest stems to the ground in late winter or early spring. Or rejuvenate plants by cutting all the stems to within 2 to 3 inches of the ground. Also prune Tatarian dogwood *(C. alba)* in this manner.

Prune flowering dogwood *(C. florida)* and kousa dogwood *(C. kousa)* if necessary in fall, after the plants are dormant. Both species "bleed" unsightly sap if pruned in spring, and the chances of spreading anthracnose in flowering dogwoods are greater at that time. Keep pruning to a minimum; these plants naturally have an attractive form. Also flowers are borne on old wood, and fall pruning removes them. Eliminate crossing and rubbing branches and remove water sprouts.

▪ *Cotoneaster* / Cotoneaster

In general, these shrubs have naturally pleasing shapes and require little pruning. The flowers are borne on old wood and are followed by attractive berries. Remove wayward growth and dead or damaged branches at any time. Cotoneasters are subject to fire blight, so promptly remove any growth with leaves that blacken and die suddenly, cutting back to healthy wood.

▪ *Cotinus coggygria* / Smoke Tree

These large shrubs or small trees produce their smokelike flower clusters on old wood. Some cultivars also have handsome purple foliage. Prune smoke trees in late winter or very early spring by thinning out some older stems and heading back branches to encourage branching. They also will withstand rejuvenation pruning at this time: cut plants to within a few inches of the ground. Plants

grown for their ornamental foliage can be rejuvenated annually; this technique, commonly used on purple-foliaged cultivars, encourages handsome mounds of showy leaves but prevents flowers from forming.

▪ *Crataegus* / Hawthorn

These thorny trees produce white flowers in spring on old wood, followed in fall by showy berries. Prune them in late winter or early spring. They can be trained to a central leader or as an informal clump. Be sure to limb up low branches near where people will walk, because most hawthorns have long, sharp thorns. Some species can be trained as hedges, including cockspur hawthorn *(C. crus-galli)* and Washington hawthorn *(C. phaenopyrum).* Train the plants as you would for a hedge, then trim or shear as needed. A single late-winter trimming may suffice for an informal hedge; shear formal hedges through midsummer as necessary.

▪ *Deutzia* / Deutzia

These shrubs bloom on old wood, so prune them in spring or early summer, as soon as possible after they flower. Thin out up to one-third of the oldest or weakest stems to reduce crowding.

▪ *Gelsemium sempervirens* / Carolina Jessamine

Prune this vine after it flowers to encourage branching and more flowers, as well as to keep it in bounds. Overgrown plants can be rejuvenated by cutting them back to the ground.

▪ *Forsythia* / Forsythia

Prune forsythias in spring or early summer, as soon as possible after they flower, since these heralds of spring bloom on old wood. Thin out up to one-third of the oldest or weakest stems to reduce crowding. Dig up suckers and, if spreading is a problem, cut back arching stems, which will root when they touch the ground. Otherwise let the plants grow in a naturally arching shape. Avoid shearing, which destroys the natural shape and cuts off flower buds. To rejuvenate sheared, overgrown, or badly shaped plants, cut all stems to within a few inches of the ground.

▪ *Hibiscus* / Mallow, Rose-of-Sharon

Rose-of-Sharon *(H. syriacus)* is a shrub or small tree, and scarlet rose mallow *(H. coccineus)* is a shrub south of zone 9 and a dieback shrub or shrubby perennial elsewhere. Both bear flowers on new wood. Prune in late winter to early spring by thinning out up to one-third of the oldest stems.

▪ *Hydrangea* / Hydrangea

Most hydrangeas bloom on new wood and should be pruned in late winter or very early spring. Prune by thinning out up to one-third of the oldest canes each year. Smooth hydrangea *(H. arborescens)* may be killed to the ground in winter in northern zones and can be treated as a dieback shrub by cutting all stems to the ground in late winter. Deadheading this species, especially the cultivar 'Annabelle', encourages repeat bloom in later summer or fall. Flower buds of oakleaf hydrangea *(H. quercifolia)* may be killed in severe winters in the north; if so, the plants will not flower.

Bigleaf hydrangea *(H. macrophylla)* sets most of its flowers on old wood, so prune it immediately after flowering in summer. In the north, plants may be killed to the ground in winter and will produce foliage but few flowers the following summer.

All of these plants (except climbing hydrangea) can be rejuvenated by cutting all of the stems to within a few inches of the ground in late winter or early spring.

Climbing hydrangea (*H. anomala* subsp. *petiolaris*) can be pruned in early spring if necessary. Remove stems that are loose or hanging down. Encourage dense branching with heading cuts. Do not rejuvenate this species.

▪ *Hypericum* / St.-John's-wort

These shrubs bloom on new wood and can be pruned in late winter or very early spring. Some selections, including Aaronsbeard St.-John's-wort *(H. calycinum)* and *H.* 'Hidcote', are killed to the ground during severe winters in the north and can be grown as dieback shrubs or herbaceous perennials.

▪ *Ilex* / Holly

Both evergreen and deciduous hollies will grow well with little pruning. Prune evergreen species in late spring or early summer to remove crossing and rubbing

branches and to control other wayward growth. Pinching or shearing will encourage dense growth and help maintain an attractive pyramidal form. Thin out crowded stems of winterberry *(I. verticillata)* by removing up to one-third of the oldest stems in late winter or early spring.

▪ *Kerria japonica* / Japanese Kerria

This shade-loving species produces its golden yellow blooms on old wood, so prune it immediately after flowering in late spring or early summer. Remove up to one-third of the oldest stems to keep it blooming abundantly. Or rejuvenate overgrown plants by cutting back all stems to within a few inches of the ground.

▪ *Kolkwitzia* / Beautybush

This old-fashioned shrub bears pink flowers in spring on old wood. Thin out up to one-third of the oldest stems in late spring or early summer, immediately after flowering. Plants will also withstand rejuvenation pruning; cut all stems to the ground after flowering.

▪ *Lagerstroemia* / Crape Myrtle

Summer-blooming crape myrtles flower on new wood and can be grown as trees or shrubs. Prune them in late winter or early spring. In zone 6 they are generally grown as dieback shrubs because they are killed to the ground in winter but reemerge from the roots. Remove crossing and rubbing branches on specimens grown as trees. Limbing up will also expose the ornamental exfoliating bark. If possible, remove the spent flowers.

▪ *Leucothoe* / Leucothoe

This spring-flowering shrub requires little pruning and bears its flowers on old wood. Prune in late spring or early summer, immediately after flowering, by removing up to one-third of the oldest stems.

▪ *Lonicera* / Honeysuckle

Prune honeysuckles after they flower by cutting back stems to encourage branching and control rampant growth.

▪ *Magnolia* / Magnolia

These deciduous or evergreen shrubs or trees bloom on old wood and should be pruned immediately after flowering. Prune to remove deadwood as well as crossing and rubbing branches and other wayward growth. Plants can be limbed up but are also attractive if left with their lower branches sweeping the ground.

▪ *Mahonia* / Mahonia

These evergreen shrubs produce flowers in late winter on old wood, followed by grapelike clusters of fruit. Thin out the oldest stems each year in late spring or early summer, just after flowering, to promote new growth. Rejuvenate overgrown plants by cutting all stems to within a few inches of the ground.

▪ *Malus* / Crab Apple

Grown for their abundant spring flowers and showy fall displays of fruit, crab apple trees bear on old wood. They can be pruned either in late winter or very early spring, or in late spring or early summer, immediately after flowering. Remove deadwood, crossing and rubbing branches, and excess growth in the center of the plant to open it up to light and air. Remove suckers and water sprouts regularly. Watch for growth that has been attacked by fire blight, especially in wet spring weather, and remove it by cutting back to healthy wood immediately. Crab apples can be pruned and trained like conventional apple trees; see "Apples" on page 83 for details. Dwarf types can be trained as espaliers.

▪ *Nandina* / Heavenly Bamboo

These evergreen shrubs are not true bamboos; they are grown for their white flowers and showy clusters of red fall berries, which are borne on new wood. Thin out the oldest stems each year in late winter or early spring, or prune in winter by harvesting the berries for indoor decorations.

▪ *Philadelphus* / Mock Orange

The spring flowers of mock oranges are borne on old wood, so prune in late spring or early summer, immediately after flowering. Remove up to one-third of the oldest stems or rejuvenate overgrown plants by cutting all of the stems to within a few inches of the ground.

▪ *Potentilla* / Potentilla, Cinquefoil

These sturdy shrubs bloom in summer on new wood. Prune them in late winter or early spring by removing up to one-third of the oldest stems. Head back taller branches to encourage branching and dense growth.

▪ *Prunus* / Cherry

Prune cherries in late spring or early summer, immediately after flowering. On cherry laurel *(P. laurocerasus),* a shrub, remove up to one-third of the oldest stems or renovate by cutting all stems to within 1 or 2 feet of the ground in early summer. On tree species, simply remove deadwood as well as crossing and rubbing branches. On weeping cherries, keep an eye out for growth that has reverted to a nonweeping form and remove it any time of year. For details on pruning fruiting types, see "Cherries" on page 84.

▪ *Pyrus calleryana* / Callery Pear

The cultivar 'Bradford' is perhaps the best-known plant in this species. Prune it in late winter/very early spring or in late spring/early summer, immediately after flowering. Early pruning and training are especially important for establishing a strong branch framework. Prune to establish well-spaced branches and train for wide crotch angles. Rigorously remove branches that grow toward the interior of the plant.

▪ *Pyracantha* / Firethorn

These thorny plants produce clusters of white flowers on old wood followed by scarlet-orange berries. Prune them after they flower, in late spring or early summer, as necessary. Remove crossing and rubbing branches, overcrowded stems, water sprouts, and suckers. Keep in mind that excessive pruning will reduce the berry display.

▪ *Spiraea* / Spirea

Most of these shrubs bloom on old wood and should be pruned in late spring or early summer, immediately after they flower. Bumald spirea *(S. bumalda)* flowers on new wood, so prune it in late winter or very early spring. To prune

all spireas, thin out up to one-third of the oldest stems each year, as well as overcrowded growth. Spireas will withstand rejuvenation pruning and can be cut to within a few inches of the ground if necessary.

▪ *Syringa* / Lilac

These large shrubs or small trees flower on old wood. Prune them in late spring or early summer, immediately after they flower. Where possible, remove spent blooms to encourage abundant flowering. Remove one or two of the oldest stems each year to ensure a steady supply of healthy new wood. Pull up suckers regularly, especially on grafted cultivars, which are grown on privet or common lilac rootstocks.

▪ *Viburnum* / Viburnum

These spring-blooming shrubs or small trees produce their showy flowers on old wood in spring. The flowers are often followed by colorful fruit that is attractive to birds. Prune them in late spring or early summer, immediately after flowering, by removing up to one-third of the oldest branches. Keep in mind that heavy pruning will reduce the fruit display. Doublefile viburnum (*V. plicatum* var. *tomentosum*) often produces vertical water sprouts, which destroy the natural horizontal shape of the plants. They should be removed.

▪ *Weigela* / Weigela

Prune this old-fashioned shrub in late spring or early summer, immediately after flowering. Thin out up to one-third of the oldest stems annually. After a severe winter, dieback may be a problem; prune out dead growth first. Winter dieback will also kill the season's flowers, which are borne on old wood.

▪ *Wisteria* / Wisteria

Prune these vigorous vines in late winter to early spring, cutting back to about three or four buds on last year's growth. After the plants bloom, remove spent flowers and trim as necessary to keep plants in bounds.

CHAPTER 3:
PRUNING FOR FRUITS AND BERRIES

It is possible to grow fruits and berries without pruning. Many an old country farmyard holds a venerable apple, apricot, pear, cherry, or plum tree that has borne a reliable crop of fruit long after anyone ceased tending it. And many of the more unusual fruits, such as American persimmons, pawpaws, quinces, mulberries, feijoas, and guavas, thrive and produce good crops without any pruning save for removing dead, dying, and diseased wood.

Unpruned plants, then, will bear fruit. But the vigorous growth of an unpruned grape will put smaller and smaller fruit farther and farther out of easy reach. And those untended farmyard apples are likely to be blemished or infested with pests by the time you're ready to harvest them. Well-pruned plants will almost always bear bigger crops of larger, less blemished fruit. In this chapter you'll find basic information on pruning trees, bushes, and vines that bear fruits

Fruit trees, such as this apricot, need careful pruning and training while they are young so that they will develop a healthy, well-shaped scaffold of branches that can bear the strain of heavy fruit loads.

or berries, as well as a plant-by-plant guide to pruning some of the more common varieties.

Much of the pruning of fruit trees and berry bushes is intended to bring air and sunlight into the interior of the plant. Increased air circulation helps keep down diseases, such as powdery mildew, that flourish in still, close environments. Sunlight, of course, is essential for photosynthesis, that everyday miracle of transformation. Sugars produced during photosynthesis fuel the plant's growth and are also stored in its fruits. In a way, when we eat an apple or peach, we're eating sunlight. Sunlight is also critical for the development of next year's harvest. Insufficient sun during late summer or early fall can affect the number and quality of next year's flower buds, which are formed at that time.

Pruning is necessary to produce sturdy plants, too. Heft a single, good-size apple in the palm of your hand; it may weigh as much as half a pound. Now multiply that by 100 or more, and you have some idea of the burden on a fruit-bearing tree. An unpruned tree can split right down the crotch, or a major branch can snap off simply from the burden of the fruit. That's years of gardening time lost in an instant, and years more until a replacement tree begins to bear.

Reduce Pruning Chores with Small Trees

Although it is possible to keep a full-size tree to a manageable size by training and pruning, you'll have much less work and probably a healthier tree if you plant a dwarf tree in the first place. Home gardeners don't usually have space for the full-size versions (called standards) of many fruit trees, which may grow as tall as 20 to 40 feet and spread nearly as wide. Keeping such a tree to a height of 8 to 12 feet would require continuous warfare with pruning saws and shears. Naturally smaller trees, whether genetic dwarfs or those grown on dwarfing rootstocks, are a much better choice and are available from reputable nurseries. Dwarf trees are only 8 to 10 feet at maturity; semidwarfs range from 12 to 18 feet. Not only do they need less pruning, dwarf plants also make harvesting easier.

TRAINING AND PRUNING

For many fruit trees and berry bushes and for vine crops such as grapes, pruning actually covers two different operations — pruning and training. Training, done while a plant is young, creates a well-formed framework of branches that can support the weight of later crops. Once the basic shape has been established, annual pruning is needed to maintain that shape, keep the plant in bounds, encourage healthy growth, and ensure abundant harvests.

Training and pruning are complementary activities. Both seek to boost the amount of air and sun that reaches the interior and to provide easy access to fruit. Careful attention to training during the first three to four years is especially important for tree fruits: good training will minimize the amount of pruning necessary to maintain the tree's health and productivity in subsequent years. Much of the pruning done on fruit trees is made necessary by neglected or failed training.

Annual pruning also performs the all-important function of directing the plant's energy toward the production of fruit rather than excess foliage. To prune fruits and berries correctly, therefore, you need to know how your plant bears its fruit. You'll find specific information on this in "Pruning for Fruit Production" on page 79.

Keep in mind that fruits and berries are no different from any other type of plant in their biological response to pruning and training. Whether you are cutting back scaffold branches or snipping away half of a newly planted apple-tree whip, you're seeking to direct growth by manipulating apical dominance. These pruning cuts induce buds to grow into side shoots, some of which will eventually become hefty scaffold branches capable of supporting many pounds of fruit.

Whenever or whatever you are pruning, it's always important to make good cuts with sharp tools. If the cuts are made correctly, the chances of diseases taking hold in the wounds are minimized. The two basic cuts — heading cuts and thinning cuts — are described in Chapter 1 (for illustrations and more information on these cuts, see "Types of Pruning Cuts" on page 4). A heading cut, made just above a bud along the length of a branch, stimulates buds on the branch below the cut to grow. A thinning cut removes a small shoot or branch at its point of connection to another branch or to the trunk.

TRAINING FRUIT TREES

Simply put, training is the process of shaping a young tree to a desired form by limiting the number of branches, spacing them well, and directing their growth. These chosen branches are called scaffold branches, a term that reflects their importance to the tree's structure. The idea is to produce a tree strong enough to support a good crop of fruit, with a center open to light and air and branches within reach for easy picking. As in raising a puppy, it's easier to train a new fruit tree right from the start than it is to correct problems later.

Three types of training are commonly used for fruit trees: central leader, modified central leader, and open center. Despite their differences, each system aims to create a well-placed scaffold of branches that don't cast shade on one another. Certain styles are better for particular types of trees. As a rule of thumb, a tree is likely to do best with a training style that complements rather than works against its natural growth habit. It is difficult to train a naturally vase-shaped tree to a central-leader style, although most trees can be trained to an open-center style. Any tree that can be trained to a central leader can also be trained to a modified central leader.

Central Leader. Trees trained in this fashion are pyramid-shaped, with a few strong, evenly spaced tiers of branches radiating from the trunk. Viewed from above, the branches would look like the spokes of a wheel, with the central trunk as the hub. Central-leader trees can support a heavy burden of fruit. This style allows sunlight to penetrate the interior of the tree, which increases the production of fruit-bearing spurs. Dwarf and semidwarf apple trees, pears, and sour and sweet cherries can be trained as central leaders.

Modified Central Leader. A modified central-leader tree is first trained like a central leader, with a series of strong scaffold branches. When it reaches the desired height, the central growing tip, or leader, is removed to check the tree's upward growth. Then the tree, which usually has five or six scaffold branches by this time, is trained somewhat like an open-center tree. Height control is the main advantage of this style of training, which is often used by commercial orchardists planting standard-size apple trees. It is also a good choice for cherries, pears, and some upright plums.

Training Styles for Fruit Trees

Central leader
This style is most often used for trees such as apples that naturally have a strong, upright central trunk and bear fairly heavy fruit.

Modified central leader
Something of a hybrid between central-leader and open-center training, this style controls the height of a tree that would otherwise form a tall central leader.

Open center
Open-center training is used for trees such as peaches that tend to form a short trunk and a vase-shaped array of branches.

Open Center. On an open-center tree the central leader is removed, leaving the middle open to light and air. The tree has three or four scaffold branches, spaced more or less evenly around the trunk not far below the point at which the leader was removed. When the central leader is removed, energy is diverted into the formation and growth of the lower scaffold branches. Peaches, nectarines, and plums are commonly trained in this fashion. Not only do these trees tend naturally to a vase shape, the airiness and ventilation of the open center help ward off disease problems to which they are prone. Sour and sweet cherries can also be trained in this fashion.

TRAIN FOR WIDE-ANGLE BRANCHES

Whatever style of training you use, you should make sure the scaffold branches form wide angles to the trunk. Limbs that meet the trunk at angles of less than 45 degrees are more likely to split under the strain of a heavy load of fruit or a high wind than those forming larger angles. The ideal branch angle is usually between 45 and 90 degrees from a perpendicular trunk; angles of between 45 and 60 degrees are most common. During the training process, when a tree is young and supple, it's easy to widen the angle of the scaffold limbs. If you start at the bud stage, you can simply clamp a clothespin to the trunk above a sprouting bud, and the clothespin will force the emerging shoot outward. You can also weight the end of a shoot in early spring; a clothespin or two may be enough weight for a slender branch. For larger branches, use a wooden spacer or stakes and string, as shown on page 11. Usually one season of spreading or weighting down a branch will move it permanently into the proper position. Don't overdo, though; a downward-pointing branch will eventually lose its vigor and stop bearing fruit.

SIZE, AGE, AND TRAINING

In general, the training procedures described below apply to trees of any size in proportion to their size. That is, while the tiers of scaffold branches on a standard tree might be separated by 3 feet, those on a dwarf tree might be half that far apart.

It's important to find out from the nursery the age of the tree you're buying and whether it has been trained. (If possible, find out the stage of training it is in.) Depending on the answers, you may be able to skip several of the initial steps in the training procedure.

Finally, difficult as it may be to do, you should remove any fruit that forms in the first two years. It's important to turn the tree's energy into producing a strong framework before weighing it down with fruit.

TRAINING A CENTRAL-LEADER TREE

It can take from two to four years after planting to train a tree to the central-leader style. The goal is a pyramidal tree with a single upright growing tip at the top of the trunk (the central leader) and a series of well-placed tiers of scaffold branches rising up the trunk.

Because central-leader training does not control the height of a tree, most gardeners should use it only for dwarf or semidwarf trees, which naturally remain at an acceptable height. (If the only tree you can buy will naturally grow too big, train it to a modified central leader or an open center.) A mature central-leader dwarf or small semidwarf will have from five to eight scaffold branches.

First-Year Training. If you're planting a branchless whip, cut it back to a bud about 3 feet above the ground for a standard-size tree or about 2 feet for a dwarf. If you purchased an older, already branching tree, you may be able to skip ahead to the second year. If, however, the branches don't look well formed or well placed, it can be a good idea to "whip" it at planting, cutting off all branches and heading the leader back as described above for a branchless whip.

You may feel terrible cutting away so much of a small plant, but the tree will soon produce new growth. In early spring, concentrate on establishing a new leader, snipping out all but the strongest of the shoots appearing near the top of the trunk. If you've staked the tree, tie the new leader upright to the stake. To give the leader plenty of room, remove any shoots growing within 8 inches of it.

In early summer, stand back and examine the tree for potential scaffold branches. The choice may be scanty — many fruit trees will have only a couple of branches. Good scaffold candidates are vigorous growers, spaced about 6 to 8

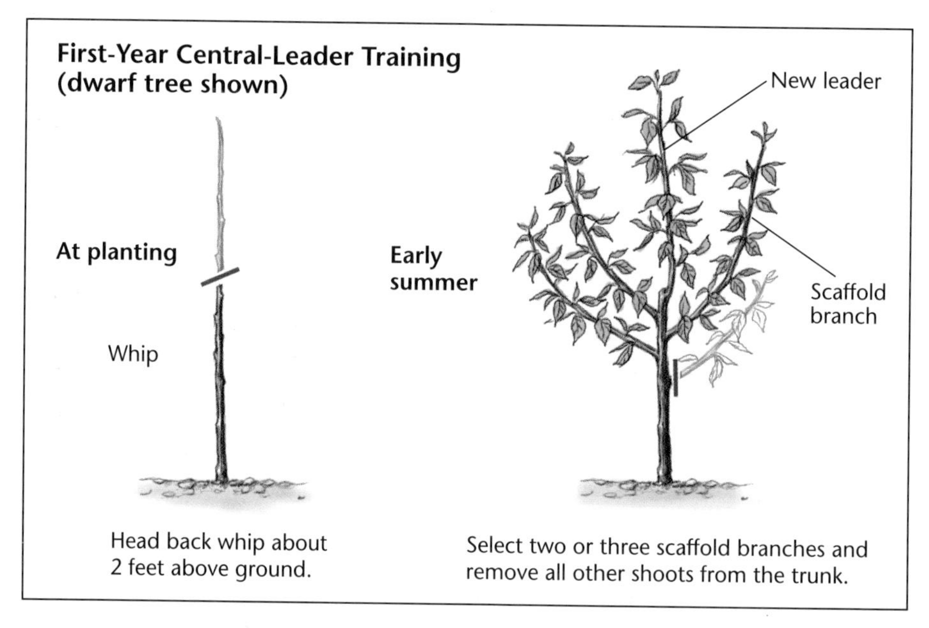

inches apart vertically and staggered around the trunk, so that no scaffold is right above another.

After you've selected two or three scaffolds (or decided to go with the only ones the tree offers), pinch or prune off all other shoots sprouting from the trunk during the remainder of the season. Also correct branch angles, if necessary, so they are between 45 and 90 degrees wide. Any secondary branches that appear on the scaffolds should be allowed to develop.

Second-Year Training. In late winter, when the tree is dormant, cut back the central leader to a bud about 3 to 3½ feet above the lowest scaffold branch; for dwarf trees cut at about 2 to 2½ feet. Cutting the leader back will encourage the trunk to sprout a tier of new scaffold candidates by the end of the growing season. Ideally, the top bud on the leader should be on the opposite side of the trunk from the one that sprouted the present leader. If last year's growth took a jog to the left, this year's will now take a jog to the right. This slight zigzag effect keeps the trunk growing fairly straight.

Also at this time, cut back each of last year's scaffold branches so that they produce new secondary branches. Cut just above a bud that faces outward so the

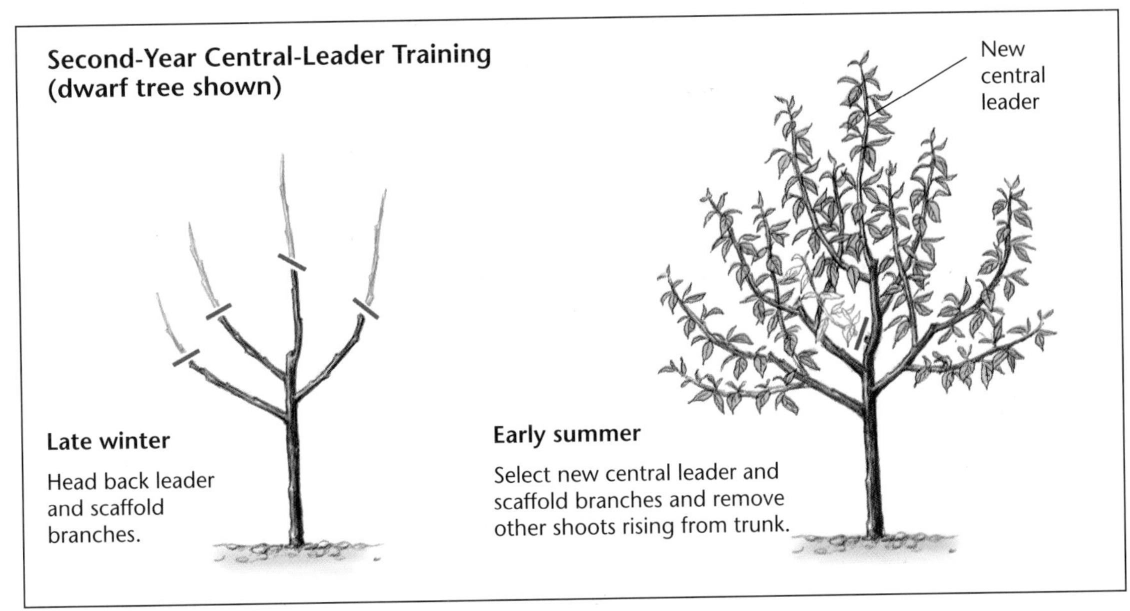

new growth is directed away from the center of the tree rather than up or into it. Consider the vigor of the branch when deciding how far to cut it back; thick, vigorous branches should be cut back from a few inches to as much as half their length, while thinner ones can be cut back as much as two-thirds to strongly stimulate them. Branches at the bottom should be longer than those at the top to give the tree a pyramidal, Christmas-tree shape.

In early summer, remove competing shoots within about 8 inches of the base of the new central-leader shoot. (Again, you might want to tie this shoot loosely to the stake.) Using the same selection criteria as before, choose two or three additional scaffold branches from the new shoots sprouting from the trunk above last year's scaffolds. Snip off other new shoots arising from the trunk. Rub off or snip off any water sprouts — secondary branches that are growing vertically from the scaffolds. Nip off any suckers that spring up from the roots, too. If necessary, spread scaffolds so that the branch angle is between 45 and 90 degrees.

Third-Year Training. This year you're likely to see the first fruits of your labors. In late winter, cut back the central leader and the scaffold branches as described above for the second year. Remember to maintain the tree's pyramidal shape

Third-Year Central-Leader Training (dwarf tree shown)

Late winter
Cut back central leader and scaffold branches. Head back secondary branches to admit light and redirect growth outward. Maintain pyramid shape.

Early summer
Select new central leader and scaffolds. Thin secondary growth to admit light and air.

when you're pruning. Also at this time, if the interior seems crowded, thin out some of the secondary branches (use thinning cuts to remove them at the base where they attach to another branch). You can also head back some of these branches to redirect their growth toward the outside of the tree by cutting them to an outward-facing bud somewhere along their length.

In early summer, select scaffolds as described for the second year, choosing branches that are about 1 to 1½ feet above the uppermost of last year's scaffolds. As before, remove water sprouts throughout the season and, if necessary, widen the angle that new scaffold branches form with the trunk.

Fourth and Subsequent Years. The eventual size of the mature tree determines whether you'll need to continue training. Dwarf trees are likely to be close to their mature height at this point and may not have room for another set of scaffold branches. Just let the central leader grow as it will. For semidwarfs and standards you can continue the process outlined above in subsequent years to add sturdy scaffold branches to their taller trunks.

Many unusual fruit trees, including this persimmon, require little if any pruning once established. Train the young tree to an attractive shape with strong, wide branch angles, then enjoy a bountiful harvest annually.

The completed framework of a dwarf tree 8 to 10 feet tall should comprise a strong central leader and five to eight vigorous, well-placed scaffold branches growing from a sturdy upright trunk. Each year from now on you'll continue to cut back the scaffolds to maintain the tree's pyramidal shape and, if you wish, to restrict its overall size. You'll need to prune to encourage fruit production (see "Pruning for Fruit Production" on page 79) and do routine pruning to maintain the tree's health and vigor (see "Annual Maintenance Pruning" on page 80).

MODIFIED CENTRAL LEADER

For the first two or three years, train a modified central-leader tree as you would a central-leader. (Follow the text and drawings on previous pages.) When the tree reaches the height you want, probably about 6 feet, with five to eight main scaffold branches established, it is ready to be trained to a modified central leader. In late winter or very early spring the following year, cut back the central leader flush with the top scaffold branch.

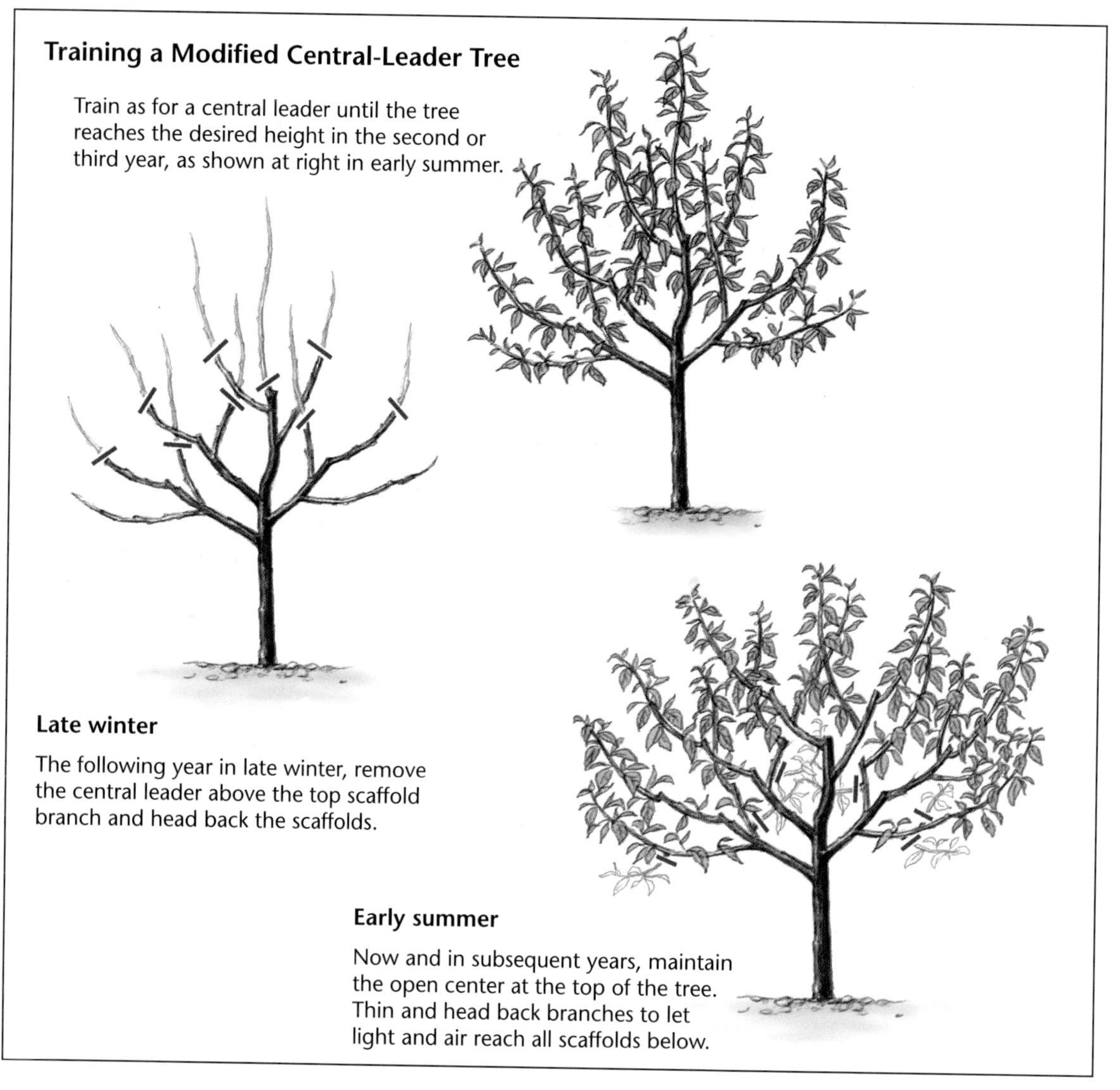

In early summer, thin and head back the scaffolds as necessary to encourage growth of fruit-producing wood, allow light and air into the center, and keep the upper scaffolds from shading the lower ones. Repeat this early summer pruning in subsequent years. You'll need to prune to encourage fruit production (see "Pruning for Fruit Production" on page 79) and to maintain the tree's general health and vigor (see "Annual Maintenance Pruning" on page 80).

Training an Open-Center Tree

This style creates a low, airy tree with three or four scaffold branches and an abundance of fruit-bearing wood. Naturally spreading trees such as peaches, nectarines, apricots, plums, and some cherries are well suited for this style of training, which takes two to three years to complete.

First-Year Training. You'll probably need to do a little pruning at planting time. Some nursery stock is already trained to the beginning of an open-center style. If your new tree lacks a strong central leader and has instead a small group of branches arising near the top of the trunk, the nursery has begun training, and

Training an Open-Center Tree

At planting

If a branched tree (shown) has a central leader, cut if off 4 to 6 inches above the uppermost branch. In early summer, select three or four strong branches as scaffolds and remove the rest; cut the leader off just above the uppermost scaffold branch.

Second year

In late winter, head back the scaffold branches to encourage secondary branching. In early summer, thin and head back if necessary to open tree to light and air.

Third and subsequent years

Maintain scaffolds and structure of sturdy secondary branches. Remove water sprouts. Head and thin as necessary for openness and production of fruiting spurs and wood.

you should continue it with the practices described for the second year. (If you plant in the fall, don't begin training until late winter.)

If your tree has a central leader and healthy branches at planting, cut off the central leader to a bud 4 to 6 inches above the uppermost branch. If you're planting a whip, cut it back to a healthy bud 2 feet (for dwarfs) or 3 feet (for standards) above the ground.

In early summer, select three or four of the best-spaced branches for scaffolds. Look for branches that are separated about 4 to 6 inches vertically on the trunk and spaced more or less evenly around it, so that one scaffold won't shade another directly below it. The lower branches will grow more vigorously and with wider branch angles than those higher up. Finally, cut the leader off flush with the top scaffold.

Second-Year Training. In late winter, remove all secondary branches growing from the scaffolds within 6 to 8 inches of the trunk. This helps keep the center of the tree open to light and air. Remove any weak or crowded secondary branches and any that are pointing across the center of the tree. Head back scaffolds and selected secondary branches to encourage development of fruit-bearing branches. Cut to an outward-facing bud to encourage growth away from the center of the tree. The amount you cut off depends on the vigor of the branch (cut weaker ones back harder) and the extent to which you wish to restrict the size of the tree.

Beginning in early summer and continuing as necessary throughout the season, rub or cut off water sprouts wherever they develop. Check branch angles and brace or tie down branches to establish wide angles with the trunk if necessary.

Third and Subsequent Years. The basic framework of the tree is now established. Continue to remove water sprouts. Thin crowded branches and those crossing the interior of the tree by cutting back to an outward-facing branch or bud. Head back scaffold branches as needed to restrict the tree's size or to prevent one scaffold from growing more vigorously and unbalancing the tree. Also prune to encourage fruit production (see "Pruning for Fruit Production" on page 79) and do routine pruning to maintain the tree's general health and vigor (see "Annual Maintenance Pruning" on page 80).

PRUNING FOR FRUIT PRODUCTION

The primary goal of routine pruning of fruit trees is to ensure abundant crops. Fruit trees bear their fruits either on short branchlets called spurs or on lateral buds that form on year-old or older wood. (For information on pruning other types of plants for fruit production, see the individual entries in "A Guide to Pruning Fruits and Berries" on page 83.)

Spur-Bearing Fruits. Apples, pears, sweet cherries, and some plums bear most or all of their fruit on spurs, which grow from the secondary branches. Spurs form during the second or third year of growth on the parent branch. Fruiting spurs are easy to spot: the stubby branches are tight and nubby. If you look carefully, you'll see closely spaced buds among the visible scars left where previous fruits separated from the spur.

Spur-fruiting trees have to be thinned periodically, meaning that some of their branches must be removed where they attach to another branch. Thinning brings light and air to the spurs and fruit in the interior of the tree and in the long run promotes production of more spurs. Thin in early summer after the tree has completed its first flush of growth; be careful not to remove fruiting spurs. A spur can produce for a long time — up to 20 years in some cultivars. Eventually, however, the older, less productive spurs may need to be cut back or removed to reinvigorate the tree. Over the years, spurs will branch repeatedly, and a single spur may become so gnarled that the fruit becomes crowded ("spur-bound") and stunted.

Lateral-Bud-Bearing Fruits. Apricots, peaches and nectarines, sour cherries, and some plums bear their fruit on lateral buds that form on year-old or second-year wood, that is, on branches that grew during the previous season. These trees may also produce fruiting spurs on two- to three-year-old wood.

These fruit trees require yearly pruning to encourage new growth for next season's crop. A portion of the tree's secondary branches should be headed back in late winter or early spring. There are several systems for determining how many branches to prune. Some experts advise leaving any shoot shorter than 9 inches unpruned and cutting back longer ones to four or five buds to induce formation of the short, fruit-bearing shoots the following summer. Others advise cutting back any shoot without a fat fruit bud at its tip (to induce more growth next year) and thinning crowded shoots bearing fruit buds by heading some back to several buds at their base.

Be guided by the knowledge that you need to renew fruit-bearing two-year-old shoots, and be moderated by the fact that if you are too eager in your annual pruning, you may remove so much second-year wood that your crop will be meager. If a branch has become too extended over a period of years, cut it back much harder and start the process over again with the shoots this creates.

ANNUAL MAINTENANCE PRUNING

All trees, whether grown for fruit or for the beauty of flowers and foliage, benefit from simple "housekeeping" pruning. Begin at the bottom and work up, using a light hand to keep the top of the tree and its root system in healthy balance.

Start with the most obvious tasks: removing dead, damaged, or diseased branches and the weakest of any pair of crossing or rubbing branches, as well as water sprouts and root suckers.

The tree already looks better. Next remove branches that crowd the interior and those that head into the center of the tree. Be careful not to snip off fruiting spurs unnecessarily. Now consider the fruiting wood, either spurs or second-year laterals. Thin or head back branches as needed to induce formation of new spurs and laterals for future crops, as described above. Finally, insert spacers or tie down young branches to widen tight crotch angles.

From time to time as you work, stand back and take a look at your progress. Consider the overall balance of the branching: all sides of the tree should be equally dense, with no scaffold branch growing much more or much less vigorously than others. If a scaffold shows signs of outrunning the rest, head it back to an outward-facing bud not far from its growing tip. Alternatively, cut it back farther in midsummer after the tree's growth has slowed, so as to avoid inducing suckers and new shoots that will clutter the interior. If a scaffold seems runty, cut it back severely to jolt it into pushing out vigorous new growth; train the strongest of the new shoots as an extension of the scaffold. If you forget everything else about pruning, remember that its purposes are to make a strong framework and to admit light and air into the center of the tree. Have faith in yourself and in your tree's ability to outgrow the mistakes you make.

ESPALIER

An espaliered tree, bush, or vine is so visually appealing that it is easy to overlook its practical advantage: saving space. Trained on wires against a sunny wall, a small number of espaliered stems or branches can provide a worthwhile amount of fruit and a great deal of pleasure to a gardener with limited space. A south-facing wall is ideal for an espalier, because the fruit and the plant will get plenty of sunshine.

Belgian Fence Espalier

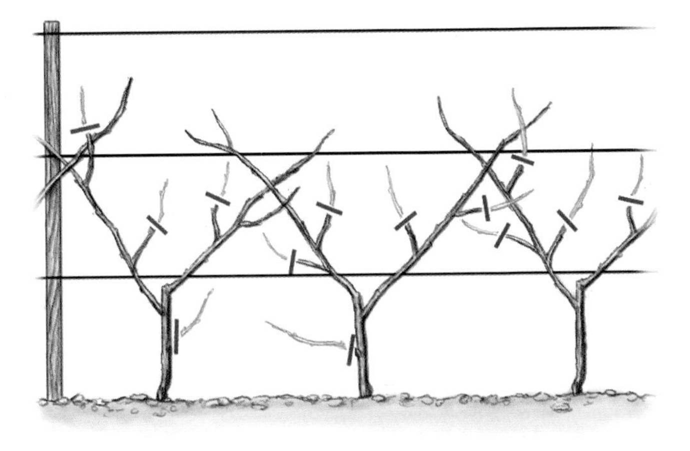

First year

Plant whips about 2 feet apart beneath a sturdy wire trellis. Head whips back to about 18 inches, then select two shoots to train as scaffolds at a 45-degree angle. Snip other shoots off trunk. Head back secondary growth about 4 inches from trunk.

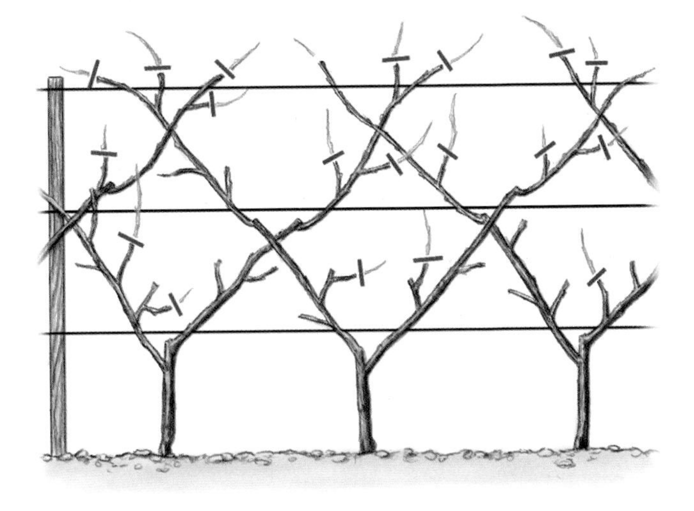

Second and subsequent years

In late winter, head back scaffolds to outward-facing buds. Train emerging laterals to extend scaffolding. Head back secondary growth to maintain pattern and promote fruiting wood. When scaffolds reach desired height, head them back each year at about the same point.

Espalier patterns can be as complicated or as simple as you want to make them. Regardless of complexity, all espaliered plants require much more maintenance than those grown in the normal form. You'll need to keep up with new growth during the season by frequently tying, pinching, and pruning, or soon the plant will obliterate the pattern and overrun its space. However, an espalier requires considerably less effort at harvest time than does a garden-grown plant.

Apples, pears, peaches, plums, apricots, and nectarines are all candidates for espaliers, as are some citrus and other tender fruits. Gooseberries and currants have long been espaliered in Europe. And grapes, of course, are commonly espaliered, although we may not think of their training by that name.

The Belgian fence shown on page 81 is a good espalier for beginners. In a few years you can create a diamond pattern with a few dwarf fruit trees.

Start by planting dwarf apple or pear whips 2 feet apart; five will create a nice pattern. (Three will make one central diamond shape; four will make three diamonds, two on the bottom and one on top; five will make a pyramid of six diamonds on three levels; and so on.) Erect a three-wire fence a few inches from the wall, placing the bottom wire 18 to 20 inches above the ground and spacing the higher wires about 18 inches apart. Three or four wires will be enough for most dwarf trees. Use sturdy wire and firmly anchor the posts that support it.

At planting, cut back each whip to a bud about 18 inches above the ground. In spring, when new growth appears, snip off all but two shoots on each tree, one on each side of the stem. As the shoots grow, tie them to the wires to create scaffold branches in a series of V-shapes, as shown in the drawing. Tie branches of neighboring trees together when they overlap. As secondary branches sprout on the scaffolds, cut them back to a bud about 4 inches from the scaffold.

Espaliers are pruned throughout the season rather than in late winter. Your fingers are the best tools for the job, because most "pruning" consists of removing buds and pinching out shoots. Rub off unwanted or misdirected buds in early spring. During the growing season, pinch off unwanted growth as it appears. In late summer, prune for fruit production by snipping back shoots to four or five buds to encourage the formation of fruiting buds for the next season near the base of the branch. In two to four years, the main branches will have formed interlacing diamonds. When they reach the height you desire, maintain them there by cutting them back uniformly as needed.

In the years during and after training, you'll need to prune the secondary growth, trying to balance two requirements. The first is creating and maintaining enough spurs or second-year wood to provide a yearly crop. The second is preventing new growth from overwhelming the pattern you've created or outrunning the space available. Remember not to prune later than midsummer, so new growth has time to harden off for winter.

A GUIDE TO PRUNING FRUITS AND BERRIES

■ Apples

Apples are tree fruits that are borne on short, stubby branchlets called spurs. Train dwarf and semidwarf apples to a central leader or modified central-leader style. Train standard-size trees to a modified central leader to contain their height.

For best fruit production, thin the fruit when it is still small. You can do this about two weeks after pollination, when the fruit is the size of a pea, by snipping off entire clusters. Or wait until after the June drop of immature fruit, a natural self-thinning process, and thin to one apple per cluster. Choose the best apple and carefully snip off the others with pruning shears. Be careful not to injure the spur or the selected apple. Continue removing any apples that show signs of insect infestation right up to harvest time.

■ Apricots

Many apricots will bear well without any pruning except for removing dead and damaged wood. For best results, train standard and semidwarf types to a modified central leader. Because many cultivars have a strongly upright growth habit, be sure to spread new branches to angles of 45 degrees or more with the trunk.

Apricots bear their fruit on one- to three-year-old fruiting spurs. Although the spurs produce for only a few years, new ones are constantly forming from lateral buds on last year's growth. Prune lightly each year to stimulate branching and production of new spurs and to thin out old, nonfruiting spurs. Prune apricots just after they flower; pruning in winter or early spring will encourage early bloom, which may be damaged by late frosts.

■ Blueberries

Blueberry bushes are naturally well shaped and will bear well for years without ever really needing to be pruned. You should not prune them for the first two or three years in any case. Established highbush plants are pruned for several reasons, but mostly for the convenience of the gardener rather than the health of the plant. Blueberries bear fruit on year-old and older branches (called canes by the fruit growers). If you are overzealous about cutting back, you won't have much of a crop. Lowbush blueberries do not need pruning, although you can thin out older, unproductive canes in late winter if you like.

Highbush and rabbiteye blueberries should be pruned in late winter. Prune taller cultivars, especially rabbiteyes, to control their height by cutting back young stems to encourage low branches, which will put the fruiting tips within reach. Always remove any winter-killed wood to an outward-facing bud. It's also a good idea to thin out plants that seem crowded with branches to open up the interior of the plant. Remove weak and old, unproductive canes. Look for fruit buds, which are larger and rounder than leaf buds, to determine how valuable an old cane is. (Fruit buds are borne at the branch tips, and the more pointed leaf buds appear farther down the stems.) Some gardeners selectively snip off branch tips with fruit buds to reduce the overall size of the crop and increase the size of the berries. Finally, occasionally thin out six-year-old and older canes to open up the bush and make room for younger, more productive growth.

■ Cherries

Prune both tart and sweet cherry trees to a modified central-leader style. (In summer a tart cherry, which is smaller than the sweet, will look more like a bush than a short shade tree.) Choose a branch that is about 30 inches above ground level for the first scaffold branch. For tart cherries, choose two or three more scaffolds spaced 6 inches apart; for sweet cherries, choose four or five scaffolds spaced 12 inches apart or 8 inches for dwarf types. Some cultivars produce clusters of branches at the same height around the trunk: Prune these to leave no more than two or three at any height. Be sure to spread scaffold branches of sweet cherries to an angle of 45 degrees or more with the trunk.

Tart cherry flower buds are borne on either one-year-old branch tips or on short-lived spurs. Older wood becomes unfruitful after three to five years and

should be pruned out so the tree can replace it. You can prune off either individual unfruitful spurs or entire branches that consist largely of unfruitful spurs. To control the size of the tree and increase the size of the cherries you harvest, cut back new growth during the two weeks before the fruit ripens. You can do as little as pinch the tips or as much as cutting off two-thirds of a branch.

Most sweet-cherry flowers are borne on long-lived spurs. Look for fruit buds at the base of one-year-old wood; some of the buds immediately above them (farther out on the branch) will become spurs the following season. In late summer, remove branches that are becoming less fruitful or that shade promising new growth. Where late frosts are a regular threat, however, delay pruning until after bloom the following spring, when you can see how heavy the crop load will be. Right after the tree sets fruit, you can lighten a heavy load by pruning two- and three-year-old branches. You can also thin excess growth at the same time.

▪ Citrus

Oranges, grapefruits, lemons, limes, and other citrus trees do not require annual pruning to remain productive. Removing suckers, broken or diseased branches, and occasional wayward limbs is all that is generally necessary. These trees do, however, respond well to pruning and can be shaped to control size, opened up to create attractive specimens, and even sheared as hedges. Heavy pruning will reduce yields, but trees are usually so productive that the reduction is hardly noticeable.

The bark of citrus trees is very susceptible to sunburn, especially in the arid southwest. If pruning exposes the trunks or main branches to sunlight, paint them white for protection. Standard tree paint or white latex paint, thinned 50 percent with water, works well.

If parts of a tree have been killed by cold temperatures, it is best to prune out the deadwood the following summer, when new growth will make it easy to distinguish the deadwood from the live. When you remove branches, be sure to cut back into living wood to reduce the chances of disease.

▪ Grapes

Training and pruning are two separate processes for grapes, which are vigorous vines that must be kept in check in order to produce large clusters of juicy, sweet fruit. The grapes are borne on new shoots that sprout from wood formed the previous season.

First-Year Training. The first step is to establish a trunk against a vertical support and create a basic framework for the plant. (Grapes are generally grown on a one- or two-wire trellis, as shown in the illustrations at right.) For the first year, let newly planted vines grow unrestrained, free of the support stake. In late winter of the first year, select the thickest, most vertical shoot, or cane, on the vine to become the trunk, and nip it back just above the third bud from the cane's connection to the original trunk. Cut off any other shoots. This leaves a small plant, much like the one you originally planted, but it should have an extensive root system and should grow vigorously in spring and summer.

Second-Year Training. The second year, let the vine grow about 6 to 8 inches, then select the strongest, most upright shoot to become the trunk. Tie it loosely to the stake for support. (In northern areas, where winter damage may be a problem, select a second shoot for insurance and tie it to the stake as well, lower than the first shoot.) As the trunk shoot grows, continue tying it to the support through the summer.

When the main shoot grows to within 6 inches of the support wire, pinch off the growing tip with your fingers to encourage branching. This establishes the "head" or top of the vine. Shoots that grow from this point will be trained along the wires. (If you want to train to two wires, pinch out the tip now to create the first tier of branches. Then train a vigorous shoot up to the second wire, and pinch it off 6 inches below the top wire during the following season.)

When the side shoots that emerge from the head of the vine reach pencil thickness, choose two of them to train horizontally along the wires so the vine forms a T-shape. These shoots become the cordons. Remove any other shoots on the trunk. As the chosen shoots grow, tie them to the wires, occasionally wrapping them around the wires for added support. Continue removing growth that appears on the trunk and suckers that emerge from the ground.

The second winter, remove any shoots that have grown from the trunk and the two cordons, leaving a T-shaped vine. Cut the cordons back to 10 or 12 buds if they grew vigorously during the previous summer.

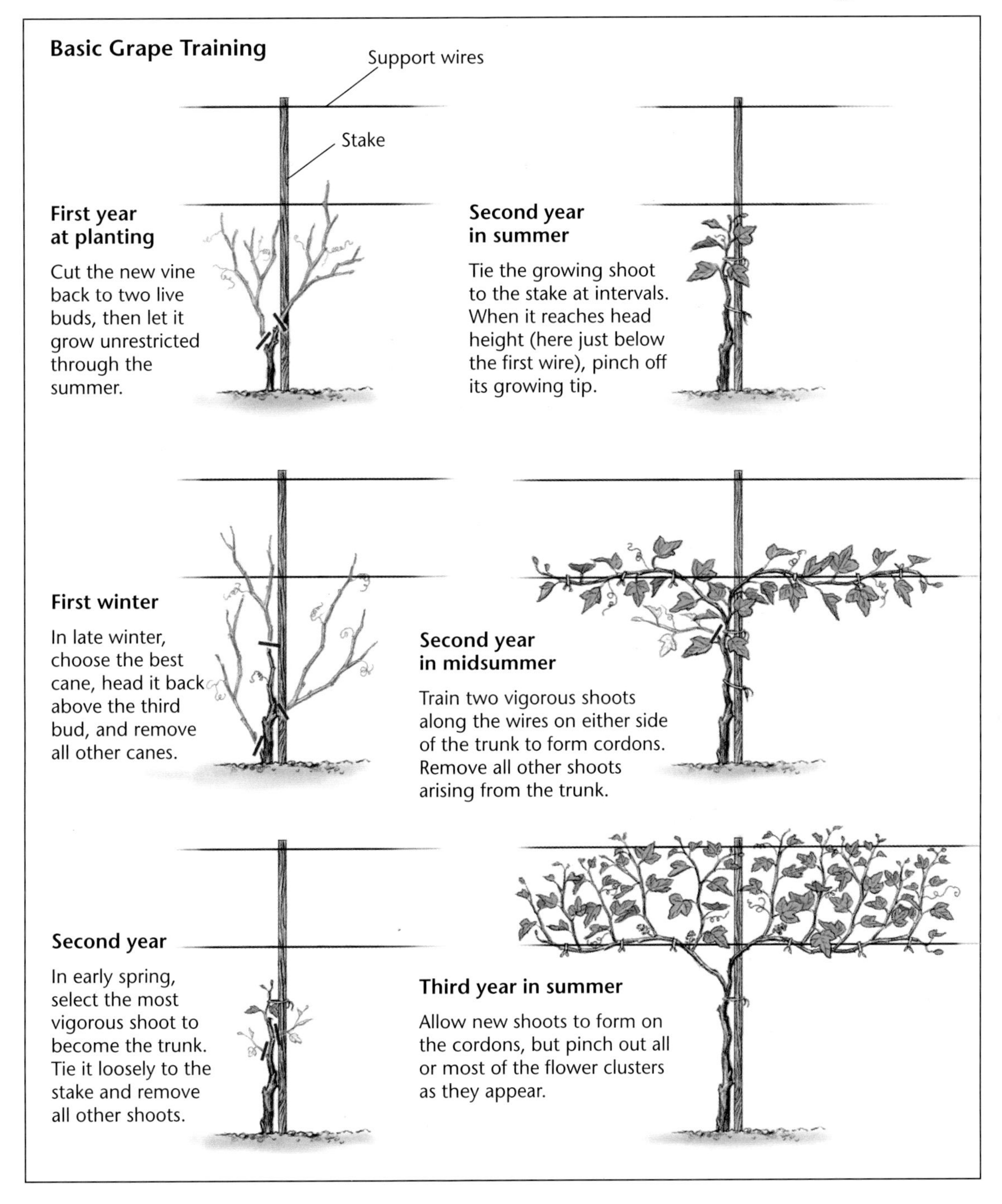

Basic Grape Training
Support wires
Stake
First year at planting
Cut the new vine back to two live buds, then let it grow unrestricted through the summer.
Second year in summer
Tie the growing shoot to the stake at intervals. When it reaches head height (here just below the first wire), pinch off its growing tip.
First winter
In late winter, choose the best cane, head it back above the third bud, and remove all other canes.
Second year in midsummer
Train two vigorous shoots along the wires on either side of the trunk to form cordons. Remove all other shoots arising from the trunk.
Second year
In early spring, select the most vigorous shoot to become the trunk. Tie it loosely to the stake and remove all other shoots.
Third year in summer
Allow new shoots to form on the cordons, but pinch out all or most of the flower clusters as they appear.

Third-Year Training. Pinch off any flower buds that emerge in the third summer. Beginning in the third winter, you'll prune the vines annually for fruit production. Cane pruning is a simple method that ensures an abundant crop and brings on a new supply of fruiting canes each season to replace those that were removed after they've produced a crop. See the illustration below for directions on cane-pruning your vines.

Cane-Pruning Grapes

Third winter

In the third winter, select two robust, dark canes growing near the trunk on each cordon. Remove the old cordon and tie the new cane that is farthest from the trunk to the wire — it is the coming season's cordon. Cut the second selected cane back to two or three buds — it becomes a renewal spur for next year. Head back each new cordon arm to 10 or 12 nodes (or however many nodes your vine can support).

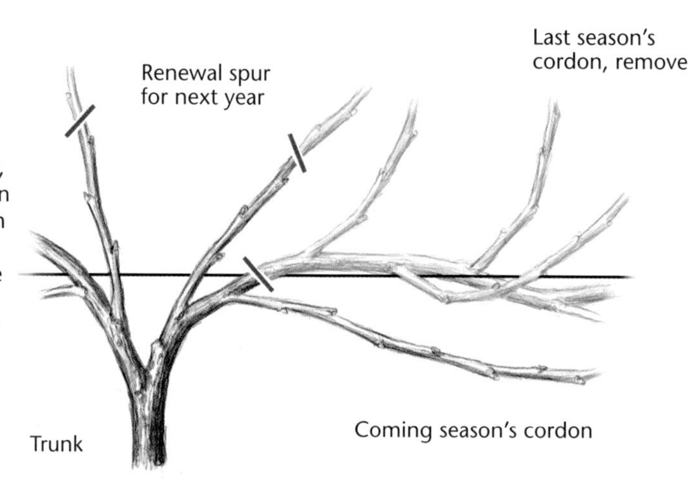

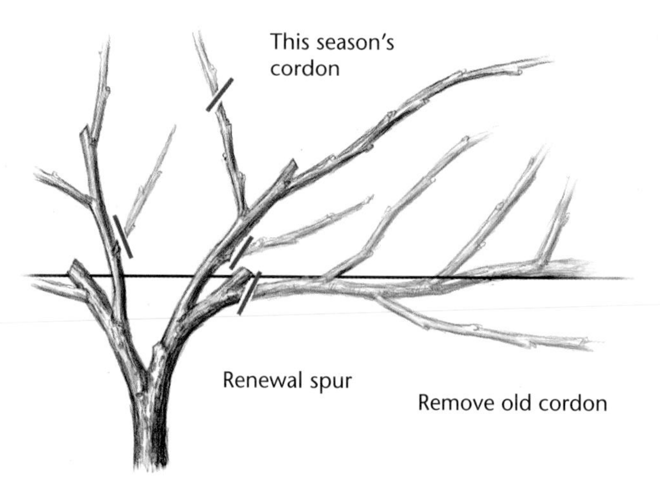

Fourth and subsequent winters

Choose healthy canes for new cordons and renewal spurs each winter and repeat the third-winter pruning process.

■ Peaches and Nectarines

Peaches and nectarines are always trained to an open center. These plants bear fruit from buds on one-year-old wood, so an established tree must be pruned annually to remove unproductive older wood and encourage a fresh flush of vegetative growth for the following season's crop. You should generally prune in late winter or early spring when trees are dormant, but if winterkill is a problem, you might want to prune later, when swelling buds make winter-damaged wood easier to spot. Prune when the weather is dry to prevent problems with canker. Make heading cuts to encourage side shoots and thinning cuts to keep the center of the tree open.

If your trees have too many fruits clustered along the branches, hand-thin after the June drop. Thinning so that the fruits are 6 inches apart is a good rule of thumb. If brown rot is a problem in your area, thin so that no two fruits touch.

■ Pears

Pear trees have a stronger tendency than other fruit trees to grow straight up (Asian pears even more so than European types). Pears are natural candidates for central-leader training. When training them, pay particular attention to spreading the crotches of the scaffold branches so they are wider than 45 degrees.

Both Asian and European pears have a tendency to set far too many fruits. Thin them ruthlessly about a month after the petals drop, leaving no more than one per blossom cluster and spaced at least 6 inches apart. Otherwise the fruit will be small, and the tree may not produce enough buds for a good crop next year. Be careful not to break the spurs as you work.

Pears are susceptible to fire blight, a bacterial disease that generally attacks in warm, moist weather — check trees daily, if possible, during warm, rainy spring weather. The disease commonly attacks succulent new growth and causes the leaves to blacken suddenly and stem tips to droop over. Once inside the tree, the disease can spread under the bark; it produces an infectious ooze that can be spread by gravity, rain, and insects. To prevent fire blight, avoid unnecessary pruning. If possible, thin branches out rather than heading back several smaller shoots. When you see growth that is infected, cut it off promptly at least one foot below infected wood. To avoid spreading the disease during pruning, clean your shears with alcohol or a solution of one part bleach to nine parts water after

each cut. Be sure to wash the highly corrosive chlorine off your shears promptly when the job is finished. Immediately burn or discard all prunings. Planting resistant cultivars is the best defense against fire blight.

▪ Plums

Plums will bear well with no more pruning than removing dead, damaged, and diseased wood. But you can keep the fruit accessible and strengthen the structure of the tree by training and selective pruning. European plums tend to grow in a strongly upright fashion and are well suited to central-leader training. Japanese types are generally spreading, although they vary depending on the cultivar, and do well trained to an open-center style.

The fruits are formed on long-lived spurs that will produce for years. New spurs are constantly forming from lateral buds on last year's growth. European plums bear on spurs in the interior of the tree; judicious thinning of foliage and twiggy branches will allow better ripening. Japanese plums bear on year-old wood as well as older spurs.

Japanese plums, especially, should be thinned to prevent a too-heavy fruit load and undersized fruits. In summer, when fruits are about ½ inch in diameter and just after fruit drop (a natural thinning process in early to midsummer) remove all but one plum per cluster. Try to leave 4 to 6 inches between fruits.

▪ Raspberries and Blackberries

These popular berries are often called brambles or bramble fruits because of their thorny stems. If left to their own devices, they will form a tangle of thorny canes and will spread far and wide. Pruning will keep them fruitful and in bounds. Growing the plants on a sturdy trellis will keep them manageable. To keep them from spreading too far, lay down landscape fabric between the rows or mow new canes that sprout where they are not wanted throughout the summer.

There are two types of raspberries: fall-bearing and summer-bearing. Fall-bearing types produce fruit on first-year canes, that is, canes that developed during the current season. Since the fall-bearing canes will fruit only once, simply mow or cut all of last year's canes to just above ground level in late winter or early spring. The new canes that appear in spring will bear a crop in fall.

Blackberries and raspberries produce clumps of vigorous, thorny canes that generally do best if tied to a trellis. Pruning these easy-to-grow plants involves removing spent canes annually to make room for new ones.

Summer-bearing raspberries, as well as blackberries, produce their fruit on canes produced during the previous season. Canes that have fruited die, but the plants produce new canes that will bear next year's crop. To prune summer-bearing raspberries and blackberries, cut all canes that have finished fruiting to the ground immediately after harvest. (Old canes are gray or brown and woody; new canes are green and succulent, with lush green leaves.) Prune out the old canes when the foliage is dry to avoid spreading fungal diseases. Check the new canes as you prune the old, and remove any that are diseased, spindly, or growing in awkward positions or angles. In late winter or early spring, thin the canes again, leaving only the largest, healthiest ones. If you like, you can prune off the tips of all the canes at this time. This wood produces the smallest berries; removing it encourages lower buds to grow and doesn't decrease the harvest. Always tip-prune black and purple summer-bearing raspberries and blackberries.

CHAPTER 4: PRUNING ROSES

Pruning roses may seem intimidating and complicated, but it doesn't have to be. In fact, roses are pruned in much the same way, and for the same reasons, as other shrubs. Although different types of roses have different pruning requirements, all require basic thinning out and heading back for best growth. Pruning rejuvenates plants and encourages an ongoing supply of vigorous, heavy-blooming canes arising from the base. Good pruning leads to attractively shaped bushes with open centers and removes damaged or dead growth. Finally, pruning also allows air and light into the center of the plant, which helps to reduce problems with diseases and stimulates the formation of new canes.

If you are hesitant to prune your roses, don't be. Roses are forgiving plants. Even if you prune them too severely one year they will undoubtedly rebound the next. If you are a beginning pruner, it may be helpful to keep notes in a garden journal about how each rose was pruned, and how severely, as well as how it performed through the summer. Then you can adjust your pruning in subsequent seasons accordingly.

Although shrub roses can be grown with little pruning, they flower best with some regular attention. Prune plants to encourage an open vase shape and to remove older nonblooming canes. The English rose 'Mary Rose', shown here, is a repeat-bloomer that should be pruned in late winter or very early spring.

Rose Pruning Terms

Branch or lateral. A side shoot that arises from one of the plant's main canes.

Cane. A main stem or branch, generally one that arises from the base of the plant, just above the graft union.

Everblooming rose. One that blooms nearly constantly from early summer to fall.

Grafted plant. A plant that has been budded or grafted onto another rootstock, generally a vigorous species rose.

Graft union. The point where a grafted plant joins the rootstock. The graft union is usually a gnarled or swollen-looking place on the stem.

Hip. Rounded fruit produced at the base of each rose flower.

New wood. Branches or canes produced during the current growing season.

Old wood. Branches or canes produced one or more years before the current growing season.

Own-root plant. A plant that is not grafted and is being grown on its own roots.

Repeat-blooming rose. A plant that produces a main flush of bloom, usually early in summer, followed by flushes of bloom or intermittent flowers throughout the summer or fall.

In this chapter you'll learn the basic techniques you need to prune roses effectively. "A Guide to Pruning Roses" on page 103 summarizes the pruning each type of rose requires to bloom freely and remain healthy.

TOOLS FOR ROSE PRUNING

Everyone who grows roses needs at least one good pair of bypass pruning shears. Do not use anvil-type shears on roses because they will crush the canes. A pair of long-handled bypass pruners or loppers with sharp blades and/or a small pruning saw will also come in handy for pruning large plants. Use either a folding or a flat saw, but select one with closely spaced teeth and a blade no more than 6 inches long; longer blades are difficult to maneuver among dense canes.

One last piece of equipment is essential: a good pair of gloves. Heavy leather gloves — cowhide, pigskin, or goatskin — are suitable, and types with reinforced palms or fingers are especially effective. Lightweight leather or cloth gloves are not thick enough to provide protection from thorns. There are medium-weight goatskin gloves with elbow-high gauntlets available that will protect your hands and arms from thorns. Thorn-resistant gloves made from cotton dipped in latex are also effective. It's a good idea to wear a long-sleeved shirt and long pants when you set out to prune your roses.

Make the Right Cut

Whether you are cutting away winter-killed canes or gathering flowers for a bouquet, always take time to make proper pruning cuts. They heal more quickly and direct the growth and shape of the bush. Use sharp bypass pruners to cut 1/4 inch above a bud that points to the outside of the plant. This encourages growth away from the center of the plant, giving it a better shape, and discourages the formation of canes that block air and light from reaching the center of the plant. Make your cuts at a 45-degree angle *away* from the bud; this directs water away from the bud and prevents rotting. Buds are located just above where a leaf is attached. In early spring you won't have leaves to guide you, but the buds are still easy to find. If you look closely, you will see crescent-shaped scars left by last year's leaves all around the cane. The small, swollen buds are just above each leaf scar. Pruning will cause the topmost bud remaining on the cane to swell and grow into a new cane.

Although the general rule is to always cut to an outward-facing bud, there are exceptions. To stimulate more upright growth on a shrub or to fill in a too-open center, cut just above a bud that is pointing toward the center of the plant. This is an especially useful technique for plants with a spreading habit that take up too much room.

Rose Pruning Basics

Most roses should be pruned in late winter or early spring, just as some of the buds on the largest canes are beginning to swell but before the plants are actively growing. In most parts of the country, this is four to six weeks before the last hard spring frost. For some types of roses, however, those that bloom on year-

Basic Rose Pruning

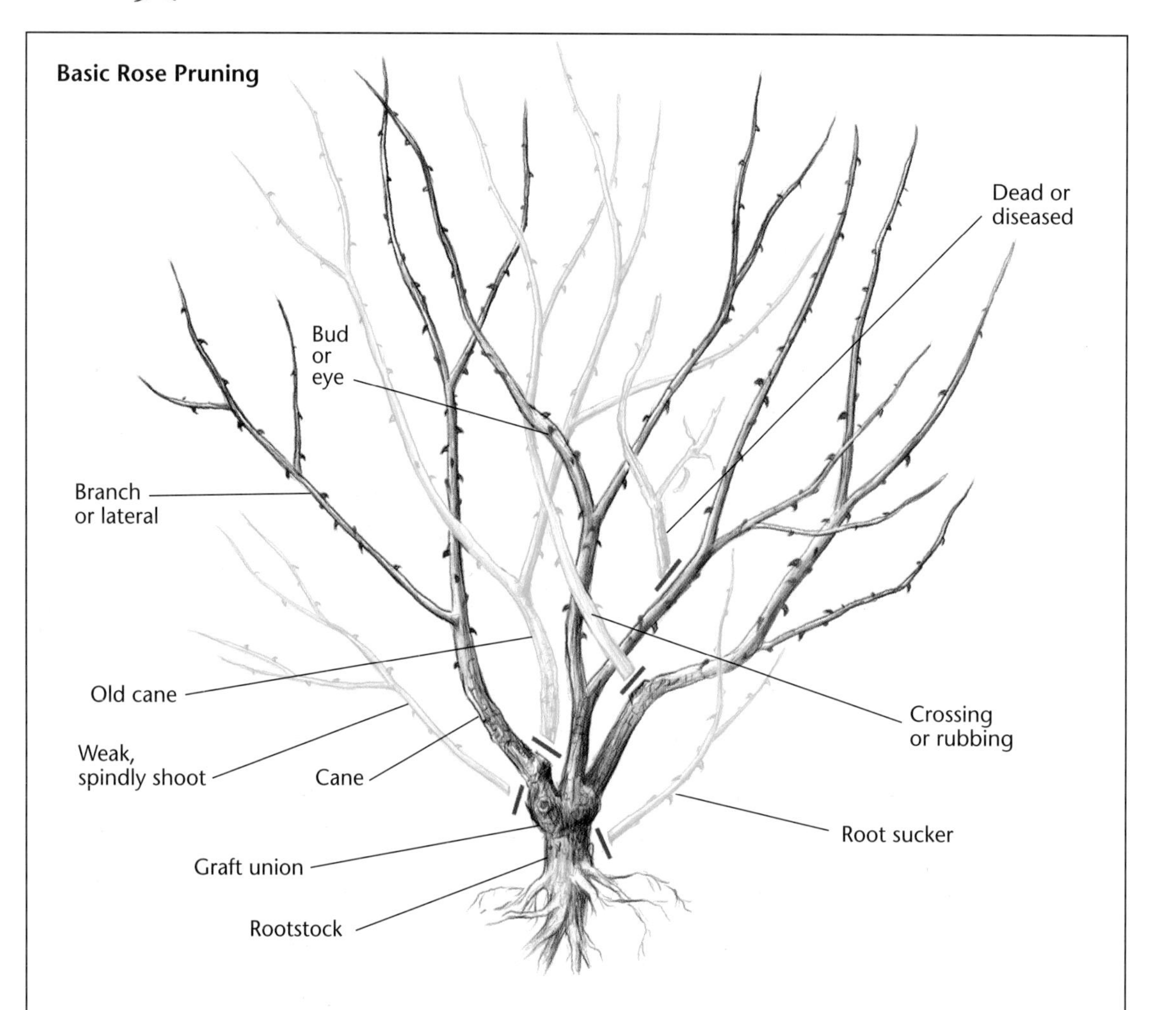

Crossing or rubbing branches. Remove branches that cross the center of the bush. If two branches rub, remove the weaker branch.

Dead or diseased branches or canes. Remove deadwood in spring or whenever it appears through the season. Cut dead or diseased canes back to healthy wood, which has white, not dark or discolored, pith.

Root suckers. Remove suckers that arise from the rootstock on grafted roses whenever they appear.

Weak, spindly shoots. Remove spindly shoots, which generally do not flower well. For large roses, such as hybrid teas, remove shoots thinner than a pencil. For other roses, use the main flowering canes as a guide and remove shoots that are decidedly smaller.

Old canes. On mature plants, remove one or two old canes each spring to make room for new, vigorous ones. Cut them off at the base of the plant.

old or older wood, the main pruning should be done in early summer, immediately after the plant has bloomed. Pruning these roses in spring would cut off many of the flower buds for the coming season.

Keep in mind that rose pruning continues throughout the growing season; it is not just a once-a-year task. Although you may not think of it in this way, cutting roses for bouquets and deadheading spent blooms are forms of pruning too: making the right cuts all season long will have a lasting effect on the health and vigor of your plants.

It's important to remember that stems growing from pruned canes will grow no larger than the cane from which they have been cut; usually they will be smaller. Thicker wood produces more vigorous growth than thin wood does. As a result, the farther down a stem you prune, the heavier the new growth will be.

To give any rose its main annual pruning, always start with the following steps. Then refer to "A Guide to Pruning Roses" on page 103 for more specific information on the type of rose you are working with.

TIPS FOR SUCCESS

TRY THUMB PRUNING

Your thumbs can be a valuable pruning tool that will make it easy to keep your roses in tiptop shape. Whenever you see unwanted buds that are beginning to grow, simply rub them off with your thumb. This is useful for eliminating buds growing in the wrong place, in the wrong direction, or too close together. If the bud has already produced a short stem, use your thumb and forefinger to gently pinch it off. This removes unwanted growth early, with minimum stress to the plant.

Thumb pruning is useful for removing buds growing toward the inside of the plant, where the resulting branch would crowd the center. It is also good for removing one or more buds or stems that arise from the same spot on a cane or branch; simply rub off the extra stem or stems, leaving the strongest one — usually the center one — to develop.

Look Before You Cut. Before you do any pruning, step back and take a good look at the plant. Look at its shape; does it seem lopsided? Although there are many different types of roses, they are of two general shapes — bush-shaped and climbing. Ideally, bush roses should be vase- or bowl-shaped with an open center and evenly spaced canes radiating in all directions. Obviously the ideal shape for climbing roses is different; see "Climbing and Rambling Roses" on page 105 for information on shaping these plants.

Also assess the amount of dead or damaged wood and whether or not the canes are crowded. And check to see how much old and new wood the plant has. (Old wood has rough brown bark, while new canes are generally smooth and green.) This should give you an idea of how much pruning the plant needs.

This is a good time to determine the type of rose you are pruning; check

"A Guide to Pruning Roses" on page 103 to see what specific pruning is required for each rose.

Remove Dead and Damaged Wood. Start any pruning operation by removing winter-killed or damaged wood. Dead or dying wood will be black or dark brown and may look shriveled or dried out. If the entire cane is dead, cut back to the base of the plant or to the graft union. Otherwise make the first cut as high as possible but just above an outside or outward-facing bud. Examine the color of the center of the cane, called the pith. If the pith is white, you have cut back to good live wood. If the cane has brown pith, cut a little more off the top, continuing to snip off a little at a time — always to an outside bud — until you have located the white center. If this seems drastic, it is; some rose experts will not cut all the way to white pith, particularly when plants have suffered extensive damage after a severe winter. Instead, they cut back to a bud where the center of the cane is slightly colored or a very light tan.

At this point, if you have cut the cane to the desired height, go on to the next cane. The ideal final height of the cane is determined by the type of rose you are growing. In northern zones, once you have removed winter-killed wood you may not need to cut the canes back any farther to reach the ideal height.

Also look for evidence of borers as you prune. These pests tunnel out the centers of the canes and weaken the plant. Remove and destroy or discard any infested wood.

Remove Misplaced Canes and Spindly Branches. After removing the deadwood, step back and look at the plant again. The next step is to open up the center of the bush and remove growth that directs energy away from the main flowering canes. Remove canes or branches that cross the center by cutting them off flush with the graft union or a main cane.

Next look for canes or branches that rub each other and remove one of them. You can either cut off the smaller of the two or save the one that is growing in a good direction and remove the other.

Finally, cut off spindly or weak branches that have only a leaf or two. Cut off any "blind" shoots, those that did not terminate in a flower. For large roses such as hybrid teas, removing shoots thinner than a pencil is a good guideline. For smaller roses, use the main flowering canes as a guide and remove shoots that are decidedly smaller than average.

Rejuvenate. To ensure a steady supply of vigorous new canes on established plants, remove a few of the oldest canes each year. The number you remove will depend on the type of rose, the bush's vigor, and the number of healthy canes. On hybrid teas and grandifloras, retain three to six young canes. If winter damage has been severe, the plant will be in good shape if you are able to keep at least three canes with three to four buds each.

Rejuvenating plants encourages the formation of new canes, called basal breaks. These may be produced throughout the year, but they generally appear in the spring when the plant breaks dormancy. On some bushes the basal breaks may grow only two feet tall, while on others they may grow to six feet. (The tall ones may break, so it is not a bad idea to tie them to a stake.) You may prefer to pinch the top out when the new cane has reached a certain height — 12 inches in the north and 15 to 18 inches in the south. Doing so should make the cane stouter and encourage the plant to put out two or three new canes.

In the north, young, green basal canes that arise late in the growing season are generally winter killed, but in the south and west they often survive the winter. Remove any flower buds that form on these canes in summer and fall so that the wood will harden. (Cutting into the soft green cane will usually cause it to die.) The following spring, after the lateral stems, or branches, have bloomed, cut these basal canes back just as you would the main canes.

Protect Cut Canes. To prevent borers from drilling into the cut cane ends, seal all pruning cuts with fingernail polish, white craft glue (such as Elmer's), wood glue, or a tree-wound compound. Serious borer infestations will weaken the bush and reduce flower production dramatically.

Clean Up to Prevent Disease. After pruning, clean up all debris and old leaves to keep diseases from spreading. Bury, burn, or otherwise dispose of them. Do not compost them, for they may harbor pests and disease organisms.

Removing Extra Shoots

After pruning, some roses will produce two or even three shoots at a bud. To encourage strong growth, rub or pinch out all but one of the shoots. Usually the center shoot is the strongest.

PRUNING THROUGH THE SEASON

After the main pruning of the season, roses require a minimum of pruning attention to keep them healthy and growing strongly. Remember the following points as you care for your roses throughout the season.

Look for Late Frost Damage. A hard frost that occurs after roses have been pruned in the spring can kill or damage new growth. If a late frost hits, check your plants for damage, which usually shows up after the plants have fully leafed out. Damaged growth is either blackened or yellow. Cut the plants back again to healthy wood as you did in the first spring pruning.

Removing Root Suckers. Many roses are budded onto a rootstock, generally a vigorous species rose such as *Rosa multiflora.* Canes that arise from the rootstock are called root suckers, and they can quickly overwhelm the grafted rose. Examine your plants regularly for root suckers. The leaves of suckers often do not resemble the foliage of the grafted plant, and the canes are often more slender and arching. The thorns may look different as well. To remove the suckers, use a trowel to gently dig down in the soil to where they attach to the plant. Make sure they arose below the graft union, which looks like a swollen place on the trunk. (Depending on where you live, the union between the rootstock and the

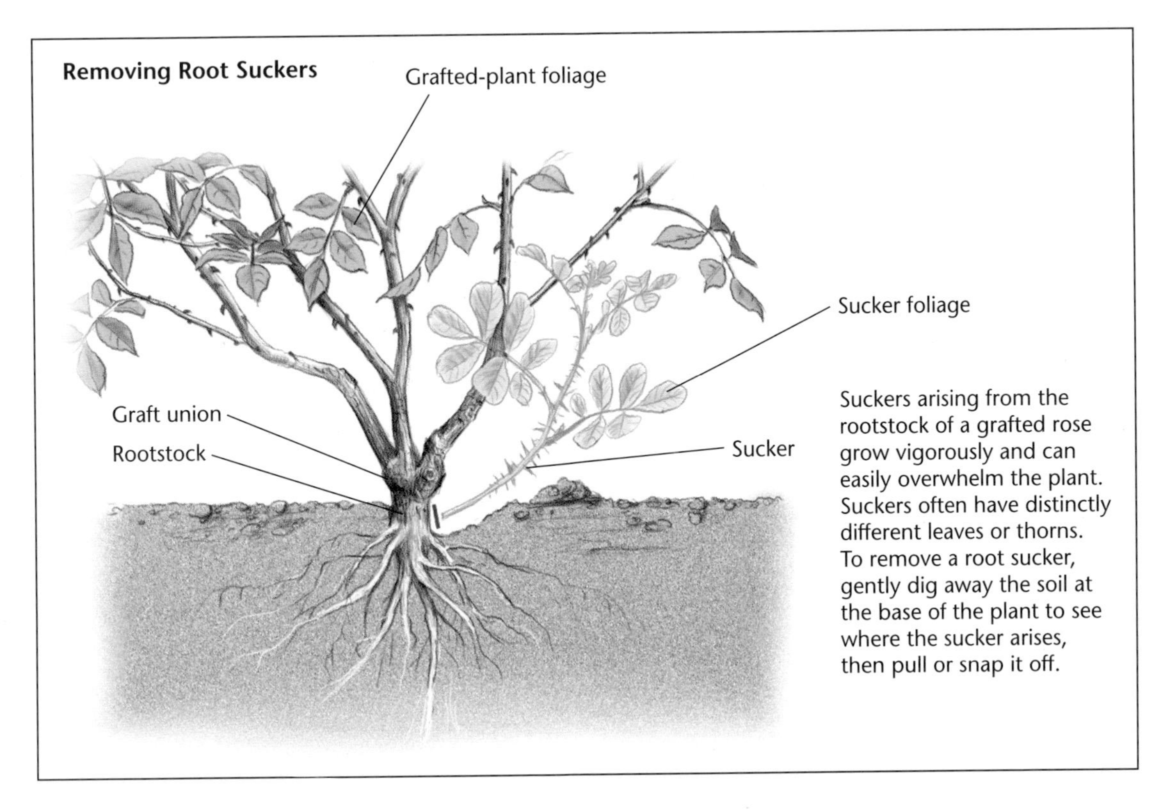

Suckers arising from the rootstock of a grafted rose grow vigorously and can easily overwhelm the plant. Suckers often have distinctly different leaves or thorns. To remove a root sucker, gently dig away the soil at the base of the plant to see where the sucker arises, then pull or snap it off.

grafted plant may be anywhere from 2 inches below the soil to just at the surface.) Then pull the suckers or snap them off with a trowel. Pulling is best because it tends to remove latent buds on the root that might otherwise be stimulated to grow once the sucker is removed. If you can't find the point at which the sucker is attached because digging further would damage the plant, cut it off as deeply as possible. Never cut off root suckers at the soil line, as this simply encourages new growth.

Deadheading. Deadheading, or removing spent blooms, will stimulate ever-blooming and repeat-blooming roses to produce new flowers. Using sharp pruning shears, cut 1/4 inch above the second five-leaflet leaf (counting from the tip of the stem down). Whenever possible, cut above an outward-facing leaf. Roses that are tall and have several sets of five-leaflet leaves can be pruned much harder to control their height. On newly planted bushes, the process of removing the first blooms is a little different. Cut the bloom about $1/4$ inch above the first five-leaflet leaf. This retains foliage on the plant to encourage strong growth.

To improve the appearance of cluster-flowering roses such as grandifloras, snip off the central flower, which fades first, after it has bloomed. Once the entire cluster has flowered, prune it off as you would any rose.

Do not deadhead roses that produce showy hips in fall. These include rugosa roses (*Rosa rugosa* and its cultivars), *R. moyesii, R. glauca,* sweetbriar *(R. eglanteria),* some of the Meidiland series shrub roses such as 'La Sevillana', and the climbing rose 'Dortmund'. To encourage maximum bloom, deadhead repeat-blooming roses that produce showy hips for the first bloom cycle, then let hips form from the second and subsequent flushes of flowers.

Cutting Flowers As Pruning

Think about the shape and health of your rose bushes when you cut flowers, too. Use sharp pruning shears and always make a proper pruning cut $1/4$ inch above an outward-facing bud and slant the cut away from the bud at a 45-degree angle.

Since deadheading is a form of pruning, it encourages vigorous new growth. To help roses prepare for winter dormancy, stop removing the spent blooms on your bushes in late summer or early fall, three to five weeks before the first frost in your area. This helps the wood harden off and discourages new succulent growth that would easily be killed by frost. Roses in the deep south may not go dormant, but leaving the spent blooms on the plant beginning in November gives it a rest from flowering. In January you can begin pruning for the coming year.

Cutting Flowers. Keep in mind that cutting blooms to bring indoors is also a form of pruning. Use sharp pruning shears and cut $1/4$ inch above the second five-leaflet leaf (counting from the tip of the stem down). Cut above an outward-facing leaf whenever possible. For longer stems, especially on hybrid teas and grandifloras, cut farther down, above the third or fourth five-leaflet leaf. On newly planted bushes, cut $1/4$ inch *above* the first five-leaflet leaf.

Winterizing. To encourage plants to enter dormancy and the wood to harden off before cold temperatures arrive, stop all pruning in late summer or early fall — at least three to five weeks before the first frost in your area. In the north, where plants may be buffeted and damaged by winter winds, cut back the canes by one-third in late fall, after the plants are dormant.

PRUNING AT PLANTING

Except for removing dead or damaged canes, don't prune newly planted bushes. Most bare-root roses are pruned before they are packaged and shipped. (Mail-ordered bare-root roses will include pruning recommendations from the grower.) When you plant bare-root roses, cut off broken roots and spread out the remaining roots over a cone of soil in the hole. Resist the temptation to shorten roots that won't fit in the hole you have prepared; instead, dig a bigger hole to accommodate them. For pot-grown roses, cut off broken or damaged roots and loosen any that circle around in the pot before planting.

Many rose growers remove the first flower buds that form on newly planted bushes, allowing only the second cycle of bloom to develop to maturity. Doing this stimulates new canes and stronger growth for the summer as well as for the remainder of the year.

A GUIDE TO PRUNING ROSES

Use this guide to help you determine when and how to prune different types of roses. Always start with the steps outlined in "Rose Pruning Basics" on page 95, removing dead and damaged wood, misplaced canes, and spindly branches. After every few cuts, step back and examine the plant from several directions. This will help you keep track of the plant's overall shape and what still needs to be cut back.

▪ Albas

Albas, which bloom once in early summer, produce their flowers on side shoots of year-old or older wood. Prune them in summer after they have finished blooming. Cut back canes by one-third and side shoots that have already flowered up to two-thirds. (You may want to skip cutting back the side shoots, which removes the attractive hips. Deadhead the hips in late winter or early spring instead.) On established plants, remove one or two of the older canes to encourage new ones to form.

Albas often produce vigorous new canes from the base of the plant, and these canes will produce side shoots that will bloom the following year. In fall, about five weeks before the first frost in your area, cut back new canes that are too tall (they can reach 8 feet) by one-third to prevent damage from winter winds. Bushes can also be pruned lightly in early spring to improve their shape and remove wayward growth. Most albas are grown on their own roots, so do not remove root suckers. Instead, let the plants spread slowly by runners.

▪ Bourbons

Most bourbons are repeat-blooming roses that produce flowers both on the current year's wood and on side shoots produced by older wood. Some do not rebloom. Moderate to hard pruning in late winter or early spring is best for shrub-type bourbon roses. See "Climbing and Rambling Roses" on page 105 for information on pruning the climbing bourbons. To prune shrub bourbons, remove one-third of the oldest canes, then cut back remaining canes by one-third to one-half, cutting to outward-facing buds. Base the severity of the pruning on

Does It Bloom on Old or New Wood?

If you're not sure what type of rose you have, determining whether it blooms on old or new wood is a fairly simple process. Simply examine the plant when it's blooming or look to see where rose hips have formed. If the flowers (or hips) are on the tips of the new growth, the plant blooms on new wood. If they appear lower on the stems, below the current year's growth, the plant blooms on old wood. Be aware that some roses bloom on both types of wood.

If you pruned hard in late winter or early spring, yet no flowers have appeared and the plants seem healthy, you probably have a rose that blooms on old wood, and all the flowering wood was pruned away. Prune roses that bloom on new wood or on both old and new wood in late winter or early spring, when the plants are just breaking dormancy. Prune roses that bloom on old wood in summer after they have finished blooming.

the size of the plant: prune harder if you want to control its size. Deadhead spent flowers to encourage repeat bloom by cutting branches back by one-third. In fall, about five weeks before the first frost in your area, cut back the tips of new canes that are too tall by about one-third to prevent winter wind damage.

▪ Centifolias

These produce their flowers on side shoots of year-old or older wood and generally bloom once in early summer. Prune in summer after they have finished blooming. Cut back canes by one-third, and cut back side shoots that have already flowered by up to two-thirds. On established plants, remove one or two of the older canes, especially ones that are not blooming well. Like albas, centifolias often produce vigorous new canes from the base of the plant; side shoots from these canes will bloom the following year. In fall, about five weeks before the first frost in your area, cut back new canes that are too tall by one-third to prevent winter wind damage. Bushes can also be pruned lightly in early spring to improve their shape and remove wayward growth.

▪ China Roses

These everblooming plants benefit from moderate to hard pruning in late winter or early spring to encourage new canes and an abundance of flowers. Remove one-third of the oldest canes. After removing twiggy growth, cut main canes back to one-third of their length. Deadhead spent flowers.

▪ Climbing and Rambling Roses

Climbing and rambling roses will grow well with a minimum of pruning, but they need to be trained for the best flowering. The canes must be tied to supports with soft twine. They bloom best if trained horizontally on supports such as wires, a fence, or a broad trellis. They can also be allowed to scramble over walls or large shrubs. Large ramblers and climbing species roses such as Lady Banks rose *(Rosa banksiae)* are ideal for training up trees. Large shrub roses that can be trained as climbers often work well growing up a pillar. The climbing forms of hybrid teas, floribundas, and grandifloras can be trained up pillars or treated like climbers and ramblers. Climbing roses tend to have stiff, fairly thick canes, while ramblers have thin, flexible canes.

Pruning Climbing Roses

Cut one-third of the old canes to the base of the plant or to a vigorous branch near the base, as shown in blue. Remove weak, twiggy growth. Then shorten branches, leaving three or four buds, as shown in purple. If necessary, thin out growth on the upper part of the plant by cutting back some branches that have already flowered. Cut back to a vigorous new branch.

In general, do not prune climbing or rambling roses until they are two years old. Be especially cautious about pruning the climbing forms of hybrid teas, floribundas, and grandifloras when they are young: hard pruning can cause these plants to revert to a shrub habit.

Most climbing roses bloom on side branches that sprout from old wood; canes that are two or three years old bloom the best. Climbing forms of everblooming roses such as hybrid teas, floribundas, and grandifloras bloom on new wood. As with other roses, the time for pruning climbers is based on when they bloom. Prune everblooming and repeat-blooming climbers in late winter or early spring. Prune once-blooming climbers in summer, after they have finished blooming. Remove up to one-third of the oldest canes on both repeat-blooming and once-blooming climbers to make room for new, vigorous canes. Then shorten the branches that have already flowered, leaving only three to four buds. Deadhead everblooming and repeat-blooming climbers throughout the season by either cutting back branches to the first five-leaflet leaf or leaving only three to four buds on the branch.

Rambling roses bloom once during the season and bear their flowers only on

Climbing roses, such as the one shown here, bear long, supple canes that must be tied to a trellis or other support. They will bloom best with some regular pruning.

year-old or older wood. After they flower, they produce new canes from the base of the plant, which will provide next season's flowers. Prune rambling roses in summer after they have finished flowering. Cut one-third of the oldest canes off at the base of the plant or just above a vigorous branch. Then cut back all side branches, leaving four buds. Also remove weak, twiggy growth. The ends of long canes can be snipped to produce more lateral stems and blooms next year. Some rose growers untie rambling roses and lay the canes on the ground for pruning.

Another option for very vigorous ramblers that produce an abundance of new canes each year is to simply treat the canes as biennials and cut all those that have bloomed in the current year to the ground or to another vigorous cane or branch. (Do this in summer, when you would normally prune a rambler.) This gives the new canes, which will bloom next summer, room to grow.

Some climbers and many ramblers will also grow satisfactorily with a minimum of pruning. Simply remove dead and diseased wood and occasionally remove the oldest canes at the base of the plant. This is generally the best system for roses that have been trained up trees, where pruning can be nearly impossible. It also works well in large gardens, where space is not a problem.

▪ Damasks

Damask roses may bloom once in early summer or may be repeat-bloomers, which are called damask perpetuals or autumn damasks. Both produce their flowers on side shoots of year-old or older wood. Prune once-blooming damasks in early summer after flowering, as you would albas or centifolias. Remove about one-third of the older canes to encourage new ones to form, and cut back canes by one-third and side shoots that have already flowered by up to two-thirds. Remove wayward growth to shape the bushes in late winter or early spring.

Moderate to hard pruning in late winter or early spring is best for damask perpetuals. Remove one-third of the oldest canes. Then cut back canes by one-third to one-half, cutting to outward-facing buds. Deadhead spent flowers through the summer to encourage new blooms.

▪ Eglantines

Prune eglantines in early summer after they have finished blooming. Remove about one-third of the older canes to stimulate new ones to form, and cut back the main canes by one-third and side branches that have already flowered by up to two-thirds. Remove wayward growth to improve the shape of the bushes in late winter or early spring.

▪ Floribundas

Floribundas are everblooming roses that benefit from moderate to hard pruning in late winter to early spring. They bloom on the current season's wood and are bushier plants than hybrid teas. To encourage new canes and an abundance of flowers, remove the oldest canes at the base of the plant, leaving six to eight canes. Cut back all of the branches and canes by about one-fourth. Deadhead spent flowers by cutting back to encourage reblooming.

▪ Gallicas

Prune gallicas in early summer, after they have finished blooming. Remove about one-third of the older canes to stimulate new ones to form, and cut back the main canes by one-third and side branches that have already flowered by up to two-thirds. Remove wayward growth to improve the shape of the bushes in late winter or early spring.

■ Grandifloras

These are everblooming roses that bloom on the current season's wood and benefit from hard pruning in late winter or early spring to encourage formation of new canes. In fact, pruning is essential to keep these plants supplied with thick, vigorous new wood, which will produce the most abundant flowers. Begin renewal pruning on two-year-old plants and continue every year thereafter. After removing dead, diseased, and crossing or rubbing wood, remove weak canes and any that are less than $3/16$ inch in diameter. To ensure a continuing supply of new canes, remove all but three to six of the youngest, most robust canes. The technique for pruning these remaining canes depends on whether you live in the north or the south. In the north, cut the canes back to 12 to 14 inches or less, depending on the amount of winter damage. In the south, the plants are left higher — 18 to 24 inches. Remove blind shoots throughout the season and deadhead spent flowers to encourage repeat bloom.

■ Hybrid Musks

Moderate to hard pruning in late winter or early spring is best for hybrid musks, which produce their major flush of flowers in early summer, then bloom intermittently thereafter. Remove one-third of the oldest canes. Then cut back canes by one-third to one-half, cutting to outward-facing buds. Base the severity of the pruning on the size of the plant: prune harder to control its size. Deadhead spent flowers to encourage repeat bloom.

■ Hybrid Perpetuals

These vigorous everblooming roses flower on both the current season's wood and on side shoots produced on older wood. Moderate to hard pruning in late winter or early spring is best. Remove one-third of the oldest canes. Then cut back canes by one-third to one-half, cutting to outward-facing buds. Prune harder if you want to control the size of the plant. Deadhead spent flowers to encourage new shoots and buds to form.

■ Hybrid Teas

Hybrid teas are popular everblooming roses that bloom on the current season's wood. Like grandifloras, they require hard pruning in late winter to early spring

Pruning Everblooming Roses

Hybrid teas, grandifloras, floribundas, and polyanthas are all pruned in a similar fashion, although their sizes vary tremendously. All flower on new wood and are pruned in late winter or early spring. First remove dead and diseased wood, crossing and rubbing branches, and twiggy growth. Then remove one or more of the older canes (shown here in blue) and shorten the remaining ones (shown here in purple) to the correct length.

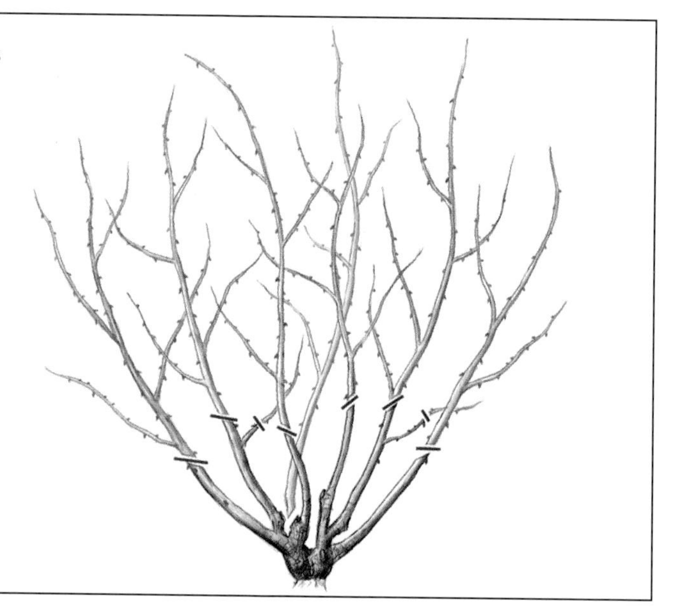

to encourage the formation of thick, vigorous new wood, which will produce the most abundant flowers. Begin renewal pruning on two-year-old plants and continue every year thereafter, following the instructions under "Grandifloras." To encourage large, single-stemmed flowers, remove side buds on flowering shoots, leaving only the main terminal bud. See "Climbing and Rambling Roses" on page 105 for information on pruning climbing hybrid teas.

▪ Miniatures

Miniature roses are everblooming plants that produce flowers on the current season's wood. They benefit from hard pruning in late winter or early spring to encourage new canes and an abundance of flowers. Remove one or more of the older canes each year to encourage new ones to form, and cut back remaining growth by one-third. In summer, shear the plant as you would a perennial after the main flush of bloom to remove faded flowers.

▪ Moss Roses

Most moss roses bloom once, in early summer, although some cultivars bloom intermittently through the season. These roses produce their flowers on side shoots of year-old or older wood: prune them after they have finished blooming. Remove about one-third of the older canes to encourage new ones to form. Cut back canes by one-third and branches that have already flowered by up to two-thirds. Like albas and centifolias, moss roses often will produce vigorous new canes from the base of the plant. These will produce side shoots that will bloom the following year. In fall, about five weeks before the first frost in your area, cut back new canes that are too tall by one-third to prevent winter wind damage. Bushes can also be pruned lightly in early spring to improve their shape and remove wayward growth.

▪ Noisettes

Noisettes are everblooming roses that can be either shrubs or climbers. The shrub types benefit from moderate pruning in late winter or early spring to encourage new canes and an abundance of flowers. Remove up to one-third of the oldest canes annually. On shrub types, shorten the canes to shape the plant and cut back side branches by one- to two-thirds. Deadhead spent flowers to stimulate rebloom. See "Climbing and Rambling Roses" on page 105 for more on training climbing noisettes.

▪ Old Roses

The term "old garden roses" refers to many different types, some of which have a single flowering and others that bloom more than once per season. These include albas, bourbons, centifolias, Chinas, damasks, and moss roses. Although many are touted as needing no pruning whatsoever, most will benefit from regular attention. Once-blooming old roses should be pruned in early summer after they have finished blooming. Repeat-blooming and everblooming old roses are pruned in late winter or early spring. See the entries on each type of old rose for specifics.

▪ Polyanthas

Polyanthas are everblooming roses that bloom on new wood and benefit from light pruning in late winter or early spring to encourage new canes and an abundance of flowers. Cut back all growth by no more than one-quarter to one-third and remove the oldest canes, leaving from six to eight well-spaced main stems.

Remove small, twiggy growth at planting time. Deadheading will encourage new flowers to form, or plants can simply be sheared like some perennials after the main flush of bloom to remove faded flowers.

▪ Portlands

These repeat-blooming roses can be pruned like hybrid teas and grandifloras. Prune in late winter to early spring to encourage new canes to form. Remove one-third of the oldest canes each year, and cut back the remaining canes by one-third to one-half. Remove blind shoots throughout the season, and deadhead spent flowers to encourage repeat bloom.

▪ Rugosas

Rugosas benefit from being pruned moderately or lightly, just to shape the plant, in late winter or early spring. For moderate pruning, remove one-third of the oldest canes, then cut back canes by one-third to one-half, cutting to outward-facing buds. Plants that have grown too large will tolerate hard pruning at this time. Do not deadhead flowers, which are followed by showy orange-red hips.

▪ Shrub Roses

The term "shrub roses" is something of a catchall for it includes quite a variety of plants, including David Austin's English roses, modern shrub roses such as 'Carefree Wonder' and 'Country Dancer', and the Meidiland landscape roses such as 'Bonica', 'La Sevillana', and 'Scarlet Meidiland'. Although some shrub roses can be grown with very little pruning, most benefit from regular attention. The best time for pruning depends on whether the shrub blooms only once or whether it repeats through the season.

Prune once-blooming shrub roses in early summer, after they have finished blooming. Repeat-blooming shrub roses are generally pruned in late winter or early spring. For either type, remove deadwood and weak, twiggy growth first. Then remove one or more of the oldest canes. Cut the main flowering canes back by approximately one-third — but to one-half on the larger plants such as the David Austin roses. Trim back side branches to a length of 4 to 6 inches.

To some extent, shrub roses can be pruned to fit the space. Prune hard if you want a small plant; prune less severely if you want a tall shrub for the back of a

Pruning Shrub Roses

Remove dead, damaged, and diseased wood, then remove one-third of the oldest canes (in blue). Finally, cut the remaining canes back by one-third (purple) and shorten side branches by up to two-thirds (gold).

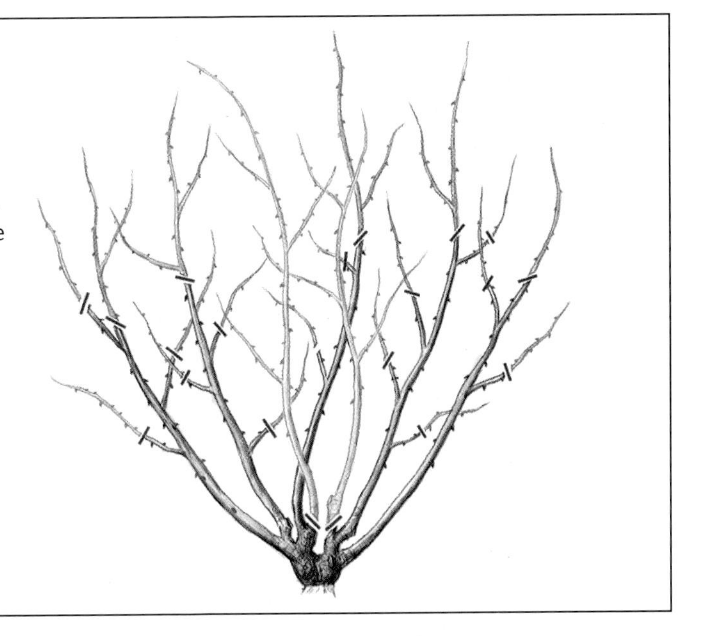

border. Deadhead plants to encourage repeat bloom, but stop deadheading after the first flush of bloom on plants that produce showy hips. Some of the large shrub roses, including David Austin roses such as 'Constance Spry', can be trained as either shrubs or climbers. See "Climbing and Rambling Roses" on page 105 for information on pruning these plants as climbers.

■ Species Roses

Species roses generally have graceful, arching canes. They bloom on year-old or older wood. Once a symmetrical form has been established, with canes radiating in all directions from the base, the plant can be left to establish its natural shape. Remove dead and damaged wood annually, as well as crossing and rubbing branches. If the plant is overcrowded or not blooming well, remove one or two older canes each year to encourage the formation of new ones. Plants that are growing too large can be cut back by one-third after they have finished flowering. Prune after flowering to improve the shape of lopsided plants as well. A few species roses can be cut to the ground and will resprout. These include *R. blanda, R. nitida, R. palustris,* and *R. virginiana.* For information on pruning species roses that are climbers, see "Climbing and Rambling Roses" on page 105.

Hardiness Zone Map

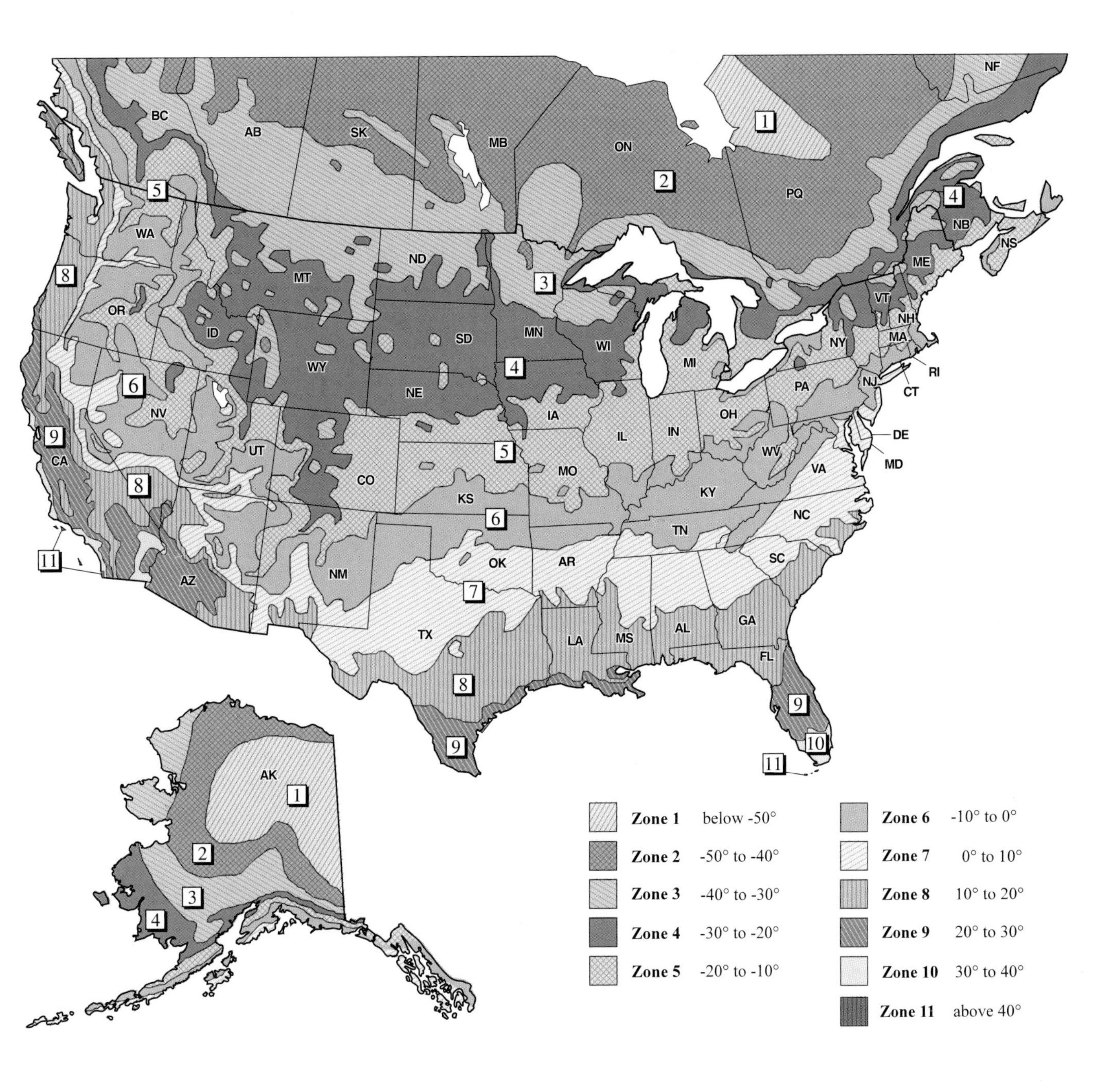

Photo Credits

Ros Creasy: 64

John Elsley: 75

Tom Eltzroth: 20

Derek Fell: 91, 92

Saxon Holt: vi–1, 2, 51, 53, 107, back cover

PhotoSynthesis: 13

Todd Steadman: iii

INDEX

Page numbers in italics refer to illustrations.